Coaching Wo

C000151378

Coaching Women to Lead asks why, in the 21st century, there is still such a disparity in the number of women filling leadership roles, compared with men. It argues that a specific coaching approach for women is not only possible but required to support women throughout their corporate career. In this book you will find:

- How to build a robust business case for coaching women
- Which areas of coaching are the most useful at which career stage
- An academic survey to discover what women need to succeed
- In-depth interviews of women role models
- Specific tools and techniques to develop a women-focused coaching programme

Using case studies and findings from the authors' research, *Coaching Women to Lead* proposes defined areas for coaching women, and offers practical advice for coaches who wish to contribute to the development of excellent women leaders.

Averil Leimon is a director of White Water Strategies, a London-based leadership consultancy. She has pioneered the process of psychology and coaching in business for over 20 years. She is one of the foremost UK specialists in the science of Positive Psychology. This is her fourth book on coaching.

François Moscovici is also a director of White Water Strategies. He advises senior leaders around Europe on both their business and personal strategies. His research focuses on the 'next big thing' for captains of industry: currently the impact of Baby-Boomers' retirement and the East–West tussle for senior talent.

Helen Goodier is a gender diversity specialist and communicator who has worked with multinationals for over a decade. She brings her unique insight on gender in the workplace to coaching senior women at work. Her current clients include Unilever and BP.

Essential Coaching Skills and Knowledge
Series Editors: Gladeana McMahon,
Stephen Palmer & Averil Leimon

The **Essential Coaching Skills and Knowledge** series provides an accessible and lively introduction to key areas in the developing field of coaching. Each title in the series is written by leading coaches with extensive experience and has a strong practical emphasis, including illustrative vignettes, summary boxes, exercises and activities. Assuming no prior knowledge, these books will appeal to professionals in business, management, human resources, psychology, counselling and psychotherapy, as well as students and tutors of coaching and coaching psychology.

www.routledgementalhealth.com/essential-coaching-skills

Titles in the series:

Essential Business Coaching
Averil Leimon, François Moscovici & Gladeana McMahon

**Achieving Excellence in Your Coaching Practice:
How to Run a Highly Successful Coaching Business**
Gladeana McMahon, Stephen Palmer & Christine Wilding

**A Guide to Coaching and Mental Health: The
Recognition and Management of Psychological Issues**
Andrew Buckley & Carole Buckley

Essential Life Coaching Skills
Angela Dunbar

101 Coaching Strategies and Techniques
Edited by Gladeana McMahon & Anne Archer

Group and Team Coaching: The Essential Guide
Christine Thornton

The Coaching Relationship: Putting People First
Stephen Palmer & Almuth McDowall

Coaching Women to Lead

*Averil Leimon, François Moscovici
and Helen Goodier*

Routledge
Taylor & Francis Group

LONDON AND NEW YORK

First published 2011
by Routledge
27 Church Road, Hove, East Sussex BN3 2FA

Simultaneously published in the USA and Canada
by Routledge
270 Madison Avenue, New York, NY 10016

Routledge is an imprint of the Taylor & Francis Group, an Informa business

© 2011 Averil Leimon, François Moscovici and Helen Goodier

Typeset in New Century Schoolbook by
RefineCatch Limited, Bungay, Suffolk
Printed and bound in Great Britain by
TJ International Ltd, Padstow, Cornwall
Paperback cover design by Lisa Dynan

This publication has been produced with paper manufactured to strict
environmental standards and with pulp derived from sustainable forests.

British Library Cataloguing in Publication Data
A catalogue record for this book is available from the British Library

Library of Congress Cataloging-in-Publication Data
Leimon, Averil.
  Coaching women to lead / Averil Leimon, François Moscovici, and
Helen Goodier.
    p. cm.
  Includes bibliographical references.
  ISBN 978-0-415-49105-1 (hardback) – ISBN 978-0-415-49106-8 (pbk.)
1. Leadership in women. 2. Executive coaching. 3. Mentoring in business.
I. Moscovici, François. II. Goodier, Helen, 1958– III. Title.
  BF637.L4L45 2010
  658.4 '092082–dc22

                                                    2010012365

ISBN: 978–0–415–49105–1 (hbk)
ISBN: 978–0–415–49106–8 (pbk)

For all our daughters

Contents

List of figures and tables   ix
Preface   xi

1   Why women? The need to differentiate in coaching   1

2   Why bother with women leaders? The business
    case for coaching   8

3   What are the critical stages of a woman's career
    and their coaching requirements?   24

4   What do women want? Reporting the results of
    our research   40

5   In search of role models – conversations with
    exemplary women   57

6   Coaching women to lead – a systematic
    approach to coaching women for success   109

7   What makes a strong leader? A model for
    women's leadership development   152

8   How to develop a woman-friendly organisation   164

9   What is the global picture? Lessons from
    coaching women to lead around the world   180

10	Conclusions	200
	Appendix 1	205
	Appendix 2	214
	Bibliography	219
	Index	225

List of figures and tables

Figures

2.1	UK leadership population deficit: 1.3 million by 2030	11
2.2	Chinese leadership population deficit: 178 million by 2030	12
2.3	US leadership population excess: 2.6 million by 2030	13
2.4	Impact of percentage of women partners on per partner profits	17
2.5	Women attrition in a global corporation v. 10 per cent attrition	22
3.1	UK labour force by gender	25
4.1	Distribution of respondents by industry	42
4.2	Statistical importance of the eight strategies	44
4.3	Factors that would make women more likely to become leaders	46
6.1	The life mind map	127
6.2	Three sources of resilience	131
6.3	Probing for aspects of resilience	133
9.1	Gender pay gap in the UK	196
A1	Respondents' profile: years of professional experience clustered by management level	209
A2	Question 1: frequency distribution	209
A3	Question 2: distribution of 100 points illustrated at a 95% confidence interval	210
A4	Question 3: distribution of 100 points illustrated at a 95% confidence interval	210

A5   Question 4: distribution of 100 points illustrated
     at a 95% confidence interval   211

Tables

2.1	Financial performance and gender diversity	19
4.1	Grouped themes and examples – the biggest challenge	48
4.2	Grouped themes and examples – advice to young women	50
6.1	Explanatory styles of confident and less confident women	114
6.2	Challenging thinking about networking	118
6.3	Good coaching questions to find balance	128
6.4	Summary of our coaching approach for Jean	139
6.5	Eliciting beliefs about leadership	147
8.1	Percentage of female executives in the UK by responsibility	165
9.1	Key comparisons between the USA and the UK	182
9.2	Key comparisons between Norway and the UK	187
9.3	Key comparisons between the UAE and the UK	193
A1	What *has helped* you in your career in the past?	212
A2	What *would have helped* you in your career in the past?	212
A3	What *would help you* in your career *now*?	213

Preface

This book is our second in the ever-growing Routledge Essential Coaching series. We originally devoted only three pages to coaching women in *Essential Business Coaching*, but knew there was a lot more to say – and to research. Over the course of the four years since we wrote that book we have refined our thinking on accelerating and – to some degree – protecting women's careers as they go through corporate life in a world that was not designed for them or by them.

It would have been easy to write a militant book on the plight of women executives or simply to adapt male coaching models (e.g. coaching the Alpha Male and what does it mean for women?). Instead we decided to replicate the formula that had been successful previously: carry out original research, both with our firm and in collaboration with the London School of Economics; interview fascinating people; draw from the best of coaching and leadership psychology; and share tools and tips from our coaching practice. Our intention is to write an easy-to-read textbook that can be either followed along a single narrative or dipped into as needed. We hope we have succeeded.

Who is this book for?

The topic of successful women leaders goes beyond the usual triangular coaching relationship (client, coach and corporate sponsor): this book also touches on business issues that will be relevant to HR, Finance, as well as the Board or its equivalent. Here are the benefits that each can expect.

HR professionals

HR professionals are always asked to present business cases to justify investing in coaching: they will find ample arguments of a quantitative and qualitative nature in the early chapters. These include reasons why women receiving coaching is not akin to positive discrimination as we have sometimes heard!

Our surveys also make explicit what women want at various stages of their careers and help HR and Talent professionals draw up a timeline of interventions likely to have the maximum impact. Our chapter on women-friendly organisations will help those involved in organisational issues to get inspiration from best practice.

Finally, we hope that the whole book makes a convincing case for Talent specialists and will inspire them to redouble their efforts to stop the wastage of female Talent.

Coaching professionals

The largest chapter is devoted to the practice of coaching and mixes theory, exercises and case studies. Furthermore, we provide a number of frameworks both in terms of women's careers and where interventions fit in an overall leadership development model (for both sexes).

A word of caution, though: coaching women to lead is an 'advanced' skill, not a series of formulae or exercises to apply blindly. The more experience a coach will have of working at executive level, the more he or she will be able to finesse interventions to accelerate women's leadership development. By the same token, coaching women is not reserved for women coaches: men can bring unique insight into how the game is played in a corporate context. In all cases we would strongly suggest supervision or exchange of perspective with coaches of the other sex.

Business managers

All senior managers – in finance and otherwise – should heed the call for more diversity: it makes good business sense, as we seek to demonstrate convincingly. Male managers should also get a clearer insight into how it feels to be on the other side: both from the perspective of everyday behaviour and in terms of career management. If this book can inspire more companies to launch initiatives like Unilever's 'Just One More' described later, then our efforts will have been rewarded.

Last but not least: women in a corporate environment

To a large extent this book is for all the women engaged in one and often two full-time jobs. By making their concerns and aspirations public we hope that it will inspire them to build on their early successes and develop as successful leaders on their own terms. These women are not alone: after all they represent more than half of the graduate population, yet many face the same problems of isolation. We hope that we have been able to provide enough inspiration, roadmaps and techniques through a combination of theory, examples and interviews of role models to 'move the needle' of confidence and personal ownership of one's career management.

Who are we?

Averil Leimon

Averil started her career as a clinical psychologist but decided early that she wanted to use her psychological knowledge to improve performance and satisfaction at work. She started coaching individuals and teams in the early 1980s using available methodology such as cognitive behavioural theories, which she applied to coaching. Over the years she has developed a vast array of research-based tools to transform individuals and teams. Averil was chosen as one of the UK's Top 10 coaches by the *Independent on Sunday* and was one of the first UK-based psychologists qualified in the academic field of Positive Psychology. Averil is co-founder of White Water Strategies, a London-based consulting firm and her current clients include global banks and insurance companies, utilities and consulting firms.

For over 20 years, I have pioneered the process of coaching in business. (It wasn't even called coaching at first). I have coached both individuals and teams in all market sectors towards a variety of business goals. My background in clinical psychology gave me a great advantage in understanding how people think, feel and change. During this time, the pace of change, the turbulence of the markets, the ups and downs have all necessitated flexibility in approach. Most recently, the emergent field of Positive Psychology as a distinct branch of academic psychology has mirrored the approaches I have taken to enable people to achieve not just their potential but also the meaning in life. Psychological techniques and approaches can greatly enhance the efficacy of any coach.

François Moscovici

François has been in turns a strategy consultant, a business manager, an in-house mentor, an executive coach and an entrepreneur. He has worked in most industries as an advisor and operator, from small companies to blue chips such as Thorn EMI and PwC. He is the co-founder of White Water Strategies and brings a unique understanding of both business issues and of what coaches need to do to be credible in a corporate environment. He works with newly appointed senior executives during their first 100 days to enable them to accelerate their success and survive an extremely intense moment in their career. François's current clients include banks, engineering firms, global manufacturing conglomerates and international law firms. His current research focuses on the impact of Baby-Boomers' retirement and the East–West tussle for senior talent.

Business is always looking for sources of competitive advantage and I have spent all my career demystifying and implementing the Next Big Thing: be it privatisation, European integration, electronic business or the emergence of China as an economic power. The long-term motivation of management and the ability to deliver

Talent globally is clearly the challenge of the next 10 years. Coaching is a wonderful approach, as long as your client trusts your business judgement and you can switch your own expertise on or off at will.

Helen Goodier

Helen spent most of her professional life in communications: first managing worldwide communications for a multinational, then moving into the media-agency world to become a director of two agencies. In addition, she also became a London University of Arts tutor. Helen specialised in diversity at work more than a decade ago. She has helped global companies embrace the subject, particularly gender diversity and issues relating to women in management. She came to coaching later, having worked and trained in a global business initially and then been responsible for clients, company growth and managing teams as a director of private businesses; she brings a wealth of business and communication experience to help women succeed at work.

Being involved in the early 1990s when large companies finally sussed the talent crisis and realised that they were effectively ignoring 50 per cent of the population – and most of it better qualified on joining – was a truly exciting time, both as a consultant and as a former woman manager in a multinational. Gender will continue to be the biggest area of diversity concern because it hits more of the population than any other sort of diversity in all societies.

Thanks where thanks are due . . .

This book would be nothing without the contribution of a wonderful 'monstrous regiment of women' (John Knox railing against the strongly female leadership of his time – 1558).

The interviews were a delight to conduct as women gave their time, their opinions and their connections freely. It was very hard to stop, as there was always one more fascinating woman to speak to. Brief vignettes of these very real women can be found in Appendix 2. We thank you.

Janna Walvoort of the London School of Economics worked with us to design, conduct and analyse our research. We are so very grateful for her patience, tenacity and intelligence in turning our first drafts into an excellent piece of research. Congratulations on your Distinction in your Master's degree and thank you, Janna.

We are also grateful to our specialist interviewees. For diversity: Rhodora Palomar-Fresnedi from Unilever and Linda Emery from BP; for local women coaching expertise: Anne Solberg, Executive Coach in Norway and Sam Collins from Aspire, UK.

Finally, Katie Watkins contributed not only by reading, reviewing and correcting the manuscript but also by expressing clear enjoyment as she did so. She even kept her sanity when we started talking about all the other books that we ought to be writing on this and other subjects. Thank you Katie.

Prepare to enter the labyrinth . . .

Even a cursory glance at the literature about women in management shows that there is a great danger of meandering and digressing: the subject is so vast and so hard to crack! The old concept of the glass ceiling has been replaced by that of the glass labyrinth as we shall see. This is an appropriate metaphor for this book: on the one hand it is perfectly structured, on the other we take the time to let our interviewees and experts tell their stories in their own words. Our aim is to be practical, relevant and as far as possible jargon free. Readers who favour a more didactic approach (or simply who want to find out more) are invited to consult the Bibliography. Those of a more practical inclination are invited to read the summary on Coaching Implications at the end of each chapter.

As we tell our coaching clients: 'You are all obviously intelligent; if the answer could be found in a book then you would have it already'. So go out and practise what is in the book: as a coach, as a woman leader or as a business manager. We would also love to hear from you at coaching womentolead.com

We hope that our book will provide one of the threads Ariadne needs to travel through the labyrinth; and as a result, the Minotaur himself may also be rescued and reformed.

Enjoy the journey!

Averil Leimon
François Moscovici
Helen Goodier
London, January 2010

Why women? The need to differentiate in coaching

The two cult 1980s American TV series *Dallas* and *Dynasty* neatly bookend the Reagan years. Women with impossibly large shoulder pads were taking corporate men at their own game and heralded a boardroom revolution which was echoed in politics from the world's most famous handbag to the fall of the most infamous wall. At the time, one of us was studying cross-cultural management at McGill University and remembers that there were then broadly two avenues when looking at the role of women in the corporate world:

- the American approach was to ignore the fact that people had a gender, treat everybody equally and fairly, by the same rules – i.e. those put in place by men over the past 100 years of corporate life; and
- the European one which taught women to recognise and build on their differences, sometimes using unique skills, sometimes exploiting men's stereotypes of working women.

This may today seem like a crude caricature, but we have all fallen into the same trap as far as *coaching* is concerned: initially we thought that coaching of women in business had to be gender neutral at the risk of diminishing its focus and its effectiveness. However, the more we coached senior women, the more we realised that the same specific themes kept coming back. There was definitely something worth investigating. At the same time, we looked at the proportion of women in senior roles and were appalled at the sheer waste of talent in the workplace. So we embarked on a research programme trying to answer three specific questions:

- Are there objective reasons to treat women differently in coaching?
- What should women be coached about and at what stage of their career?
- Are there any techniques and approaches that work particularly well when coaching women?

We attempted to answer these questions in the specific context of a corporate environment and in coaching women to have a career progression that allowed them to express their full potential – i.e. get to leadership positions comparable to that of equally qualified men. We took three approaches:

- We built a robust business case to demonstrate that coaching women to lead is clearly worth the effort.
- We did the obvious to find out about needs: we asked women!
- We also trawled the world for examples of gender-specific coaching, looked at our own practice and asked coached women what had been the most useful in their own coaching.

This book is the result of this research. We start from the general (is it worth it?) to the specific (tools and techniques). It is organised as follows:

Chapter 2: Why bother with women leaders? The business case for coaching

The corporate world likes nothing better than a solid business case. Although one could make a moral case for some form of affirmative action to increase the proportion of women in leadership positions, it is not nearly as strong as pounds and pence (or your preferred currency). If coaching is effective at increasing the number of successful women leaders, then is it worth the time and cost? In this chapter you will learn:

- why most economies – East and West – face a 'leadership cliff' and how women could help make up this leadership deficit;
- the cash benefits of gender diversity; and
- how to calculate the value of actively managing the pipeline of women leaders to increase talent retention and save recruitment and associated costs.

By the end of this chapter you should be able to draw up a solid set of arguments for your own business environment and articulate how an investment in coaching can play a role not only in promoting existing women to leadership positions but also in attracting both new and returning women to your organisation.

Chapter 3: What are the critical stages of a woman's career and their coaching requirements?

All managers have important career stages that require specific coaching interventions: the first big promotion into a visible leadership role and mid-career relaunch are quasi-universal experiences. Women have additional specific coaching needs linked to the child-bearing years (a.k.a. off-ramping/on-ramping for our US colleagues) and gaining boardroom access. In this chapter we look at a typical corporate career and analyse key career stages and associated coaching interventions.

By the end of this chapter emerging women leaders should have a good sense of the successive decisions they have to consider when planning their career (managing the so-called glass labyrinth) and how coaching can help in each case. Coaches will find it easier to plan their interventions using this chapter as a roadmap. Business managers will have a deeper understanding of the key stages at which they lose female staff and what they can do about them.

Chapter 4: What do women want? Reporting the results of our research

This is the chapter that analyses research commissioned specifically for this book. We have developed and conducted a questionnaire in association with the London School of Economics and present statistically significant results as well as many quotes and words of advice from respondents. In this chapter you will find:

- the perceived key drivers of success for women in a corporate environment;
- the biggest challenges at all levels;
- advice given to other women in a corporate context in all areas including confidence, gender behaviour, career strategies, emotional advice, etc.;
- coaching implications.

Chapter 5: In search of role models – conversations with exemplary women

We have carried out 25 in-depth interviews of women in senior positions who, by any standard, have 'made it'. They share their story and dispense advice liberally. Our aim here was to identify and distil the wisdom of genuine role models – not merely women who were successful by playing by the men's rules.

We provide the transcripts of 14 conversations with senior women with minimum interference: the feedback from our previous book using this format was that readers really enjoyed the immediacy of the conversations and could better relate to the situations than if they had been summarised and sanitised. Anecdotes range from defining moments in their careers to reflecting on lessons for today's young managers. They also describe what type of coaching they received along the way (if any), how it helped them; and they express views on the best timing for coaching.

Chapter 6: Coaching women to lead – a systematic approach to coaching women for success

For coaches this is the key chapter of the book: we draw from the knowledge of all that precedes, and add our own experience in cognitive behavioural coaching at a senior level to reveal key interventions. In each section you will find a summary of the issue, the psychological underpinnings where relevant, several coaching exercises and an illustrative case study. The themes covered are:

- confidence
- networking
- role models
- balancing career and family
- resilience
- navigating the labyrinth
- playing the game
- developing presence
- developing into a leader.

Chapter 7: What makes a strong leader? A model for women's leadership development

If women require specific coaching interventions they also require excellent general leadership coaching. In this chapter we re-examine what makes a good leader. We expand on our ITEA model first presented in *Essential Business Coaching* and enrich it with recent research that looks at eight long-term characteristics for emerging and confirmed leaders. We call our new model the Balanced Leader and for each characteristic we point out any gender-specific issue and the coaching approach to deal with it. This can be seen as a long-term road map for all leaders to follow. According to our research, Balanced Leaders are:

- visible
- resilient
- strategic
- emotional
- decisive
- intellectual
- behavioural
- meaningful.

Chapter 8: How to develop a woman-friendly organisation

What should be clear by now is that women-friendly organisations are more likely to attract and retain good quality women managers – as well as enable them to progress to very senior levels including the boardroom; and that there is a business case for creating such organisations. This chapter feeds from our existing expertise in designing diversity-friendly environments as well as from the specific recommendations collected in our survey and our interviews. It makes the distinction between the organisations that pile policy upon policy and those that have the courage to start again from scratch. We make our recommendations in the context of historical achievements as well as recent research by leading think tanks. Finally, we consider what women can do for themselves while (not) waiting for the perfect organisation to emerge.

Chapter 9: What is the global picture? Lessons from coaching women to lead around the world

If the grass is always greener on the other side of the fence, could we learn something from how women are coached to lead in other countries? Also, when we are coaching women from different backgrounds and cultures, should we pay specific attention to aspects of their culture and perspective on leadership? This chapter takes us on a three-country trip and then back to the UK: we examine the social background as well as coaching practices in the USA, Norway and the Middle East and draw comparisons with the UK. We highlight differences in the context of the universal experiences that women go through on their way to the top.

Chapter 10: Conclusions

We started off with a potentially controversial question: Do we need to consider specific and different coaching for women? You can go straight to this chapter and find out the answer, or enjoy the journey and read the book first!

We summarise our findings about when and how to coach, and the skills that leadership coaches working with women should acquire. We also consider what else women need to flourish in a corporate environment, and what benefits employers can expect when they reach the tipping point in terms of grooming women leaders in the right quantity and quality. We also look at the role that men have to play in making it all happen.

Our conclusions extend beyond coaching, looking at organisation design and the bigger picture of Talent Management. Finally we suggest new areas for research and practice.

Show me . . .

This book aims to debunk many myths about women and leadership; it is largely about showing through commissioned and external research why and how coaching can have a huge impact. So we shall start with the obvious in the next chapter: 'Show me the money . . .'

Why bother with women leaders? The business case for coaching

'I do not wish them to have power over men; but over themselves.'

Mary Wollstonecraft

January 1st, 2011

This is the first official date when Baby Boomers, the generation born between 1946 and 1965, start to retire. In practice, this started some time ago. The actual proportion of people in employment toward the end of the official retiring age in most countries has dropped dramatically since 1950. According to the OECD, fewer than 60 per cent of 50–64 year olds are working (compared to 76 per cent of 24–49 year olds). Specifically, only 47 per cent of Americans aged 60–64 are working in 2010. This drops to 38 per cent in the UK, 32 per cent in Germany and an amazing 14 per cent in France. This is due to a number of hard-to-reverse factors such as early retirement provisions by industry, or severe pension and tax penalties if you wish to continue working. So many of our existing leaders will soon be gone and, put simply, we did not make enough babies 30 years ago to replace them.

This chapter makes the very real business case for developing women into leadership positions and retaining them in management along two key arguments:

- The war for talent is intensifying as the demographics projections become a reality around the word, including emerging markets. This demographic attrition is only one of several drivers that are weakening the ability of corporations around the world. We will demonstrate that they are literally walking towards a Leadership Cliff. Engaging more women into senior leadership ranks is one of the ways to solve a long-term problem. We call this *Surviving the Leadership Cliff.*

• Companies with more women at the top actually do better than those that don't have them. It is therefore good business practice to help women to reach the top. We call this *Building the Leadership-Rich Corporation.*

We also look at the actual typical life cycle of women in management positions and propose key points of loss or gain where companies can take action, such as coaching, which will have a significant effect on the attraction and retention of women with a corresponding effect on financial performance. In other words, we make the case for the return on coaching investment when supporting emerging women leaders. We are using coaching to *Manage the Leadership Pipeline.*

This book uses the corporation as a generic descriptor for large businesses and comparable public sector or not-for-profit organisations. We treat owner-managed businesses and other forms of occupation as alternatives to the corporate model. To a large extent, the Leadership Cliff is a corporate problem concerned with attracting and retaining quality leaders in a traditional employment setting.

Surviving the Leadership Cliff

Demographics and economic growth

The beauty about demographics is that you can see them coming from a long way away. The first alarm concerning management and demographics was raised in 1997 in the *McKinsey Quarterly* (the famous War for Talent article; Chambers, Foulon, Handfield-Jones, Hankin and Michaels, 1998; and see Michaels, Handfield-Jones and Axelrod, 2001 for followup publication). However, this was before the realisation that China would soon become the world's largest economy, before India's embrace of capitalism or before the population decline in the former Soviet Union. We have revised the United Nations' projections on age pyramids around the world and compared them to expected management needs and made some interesting discoveries: in brief, the industrial world will be short of ~ 200 million individuals of leadership age by 2030!

If we make the rough assumption that one person per hundred in the 30–44 age bracket assumes some sort of leadership position, then the world will be short of 2 million leaders by 2030. Let us examine this in greater detail:

- The shape of the population pyramid in each country is predictable and stable. Although localised immigration is possible, this can be very transient – witness the large influx and subsequent outflow of Polish workers in the UK in the last 10 years for example.
- There is a long-term correlation between GDP growth and employment needs: if the economy grows by 10 per cent in real terms, you will need 10 per cent more workers and consumers to produce and absorb the change. This holds true around the world, even when taking productivity gains into account. When using long time series we smooth out distortions of local economic crises – we have analysed 18 years of data.
- We consider the 30–44 age bracket to be key when identifying leadership trends, as it is this age group that is 'in charge' of gradually replacing the Baby Boomers. We wanted to know if there would be enough of them around.

The results of our analysis are somewhat shocking and counterintuitive:

- Most European countries will experience a significant gap between leadership-age population supply and demand driven by economic growth. Even relatively high-birth-rate countries such as France will come up short. Figures 2.1– 2.3 illustrate the gaps: the UK will be short of 1.3 million people in the 30–44 age bracket by 2030, France 1.6 million and Germany a significant 3.4 million. Assuming that about 1 per cent of this shortage is for people in leadership positions, this means that Europe's three largest

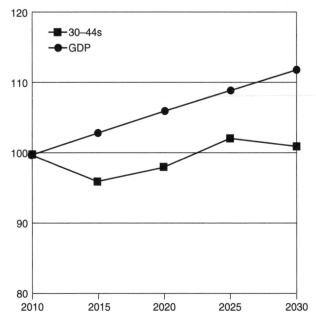

Figure 2.1 **UK leadership population deficit: 1.3 million by 2030**

economies will need 60,000 'missing' leaders across all
sectors.

- Any hope of importing leadership from Asia along with
  the usual manufacturing goods should be dashed: Japan
  is ageing almost terminally and will be short of almost
  10 million people in the 30–44 age bracket. The big shock
  however comes from China: with the one-child policy
  working its way through the ranks, the country will be
  short of a staggering 178 million people!
- India will be the only country with a modest positive
  balance (+25 million), but this could quickly be absorbed
  if economic growth keeps accelerating much above the
  historic trend we used for the analysis.
- Oddly enough the country that started the Baby Boomer
  retirement scare, the USA, will fare fairly well, at least
  over 2010–2020. The positive gap thins out to 2.6 million by
  the end of the forecast period, casting doubt on the ability

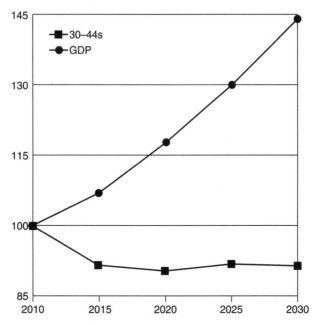

Figure 2.2 Chinese leadership population deficit: 178 million by 2030

of the USA to act as a net exporter of leaders to the rest of the world. Other high immigration countries such as Canada and Australia show a good balance between projected supply and expected demand over the forecast period.

So we can now answer the first part of our question: 'Where have all the leaders gone?' They have retired and will not be replaced, at least not by younger *men*, especially in Asia and in Europe. But demographics are only one component of the Leadership Cliff.

Sleepwalking towards the edge of the Leadership Cliff

Corporations (and governments) are facing two further battlefronts: retaining employees and engaging them in order to benefit from the efforts of a motivated and productive

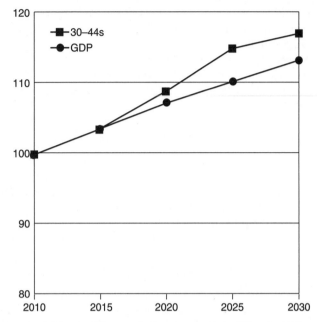

Figure 2.3 **US leadership population excess: 2.6 million by 2030**

workforce. There is evidence that they are failing on both counts and things are getting worse.

Survey after survey confirms what we suspected: most employees are sleepwalking to work. Comprehensive global studies by Towers Perrin (now Towers Watson; *Global Workforce Study* 2007/08, 2009/10) demonstrate year after year that only 1 employee in 10 is highly engaged in their job. If we are doing such a poor job engaging current employees – those who are of the same generation as us – how can we expect to motivate and keep in a corporate environment younger generations who have seen their parents being 'de-layered' in the 1990s, who do not subscribe to the dreams of greed and shoulder pads, and who put engagement and personal development at the top of their priority list when looking for a job? It is not in the scope of this book to discuss how to engage Generation X and Generation Y in a corporate environment; suffice to say that a sizeable proportion of young leaders are choosing to work outside the traditional corporate world and that this is compounding the demographic problem.

A number of other factors are complicating the picture and creating local imbalances between supply and demand for leaders, at least in a localised fashion. Let us examine some of them.

Consolidation of the 'Mittelstandt' across Europe

The second generation of postwar small businesses are retiring at the same time as the Baby Boomers. Some companies will continue as family businesses or close down but many will be bought out and consolidated into larger companies, increasing demand for leaders in a corporate environment. This is true in Germany, Italy and Switzerland for example.

Emergence of the transnational corporation to replace the multinational corporation

Technology and globalisation of supply chains now allow large multinationals to be redesigned along global centres of competence: IBM has announced for example that their whole manufacturing function was moving to China, including all senior management. This new organisational mode will shift demand for leaders to new countries where they will have to fight for talent with established family businesses (e.g. in India) or fish from a shrinking talent pool (e.g. in China).

South-to-north and east-to-west mergers and acquisitions activity

There has been a remarkable change of direction in European mergers and acquisitions over the past 10 years – who would have thought for example that Spain and Russia would be key players in the acquisition of major infrastructure players, traditionally the turf of national champions? Human nature is such that owners tend to prefer senior managers of the same nationality as that of the home base. This puts a premium on leaders who are multilingual and prepared to travel, further putting pressure on supply. The next stage in this shift is the emergence of new global brands from China and India. This is already starting in household goods (China) and cars (India) for example. Who will be managing Chinese businesses in Europe and America, especially given the shortage of Chinese executives? This is likely to further deplete the availability of non-Chinese executives – or will the nationality of origin argument prevail? Nobody knows, but disruption is likely.

The acceleration of private equity

The credit crunch has put a stop to easy or highly leveraged money, but this is typically a pause. We expect the long term trend for increased private equity participation in the economy to resume. A strong argument is that Generation Y upcoming leaders also known as 'the children of divorce' are more independent, resilient and flexible than their parents. We expect them to embrace different organisational models. Private equity will help them escape corporate life, further diminishing the pool of available talent to corporations and governments.

Stepping away from the edge of the Cliff: engaging Non-Participants

The Leadership Cliff is a simple problem of supply and demand. It should be clear by now that we are well on our way to major supply problems that cannot be solved by importing a handful of executives from another country or by paying people more: any arms race in that area is bound to fail. Our argument is that only those companies that find a way to tap into other resources will succeed. The next question obviously becomes: who are the Non-Participants in the leadership pool?

An obvious group is recently retired executives. The simple extension of retirement ages will go some way to address the long-term problem of leadership availability, but this will not help in the next 10–20 years: the Boomers have already retired or are about to do so! We are currently researching the engagement of 'Gray Hairs' but this is still work in progress. By far the largest under-represented group in corporations is women. Although this is instinctively true (a cursory look at any airline first-class lounge is a good proxy for the proportion of women to men in the boardroom), let us consider some key numbers:

- We know that women do well at school and this includes training in the professions: young women make up 62 per cent of law graduates in the UK for example, as well as 53 per cent of newly qualified doctors in Canada. In the USA, they marginally outnumber men in junior professional and management roles 51/49.
- However, when we turn to senior ranks the picture is markedly different: if 15 per cent of Fortune 500 Board Directors are women, the vast majority are non-executives and only 1.6 per cent of CEOs are women. If you strip away the fashion and retail sectors the numbers become minute.
- Things are not much better in the professions: although women represent 30–40 per cent of accountants qualified by the Big Four audit firms in the UK, their proportion of women partners stagnates at 10–15 per cent.

So there you have it: corporations need more leaders, women could be available to switch from Non-Participants to Participants, so why is this not happening? An obvious question to ask is whether having more women at the top helps companies perform better. This is the object of the next section.

Building the leadership-rich corporation

Cash benefits of gender diversity

If you start from the premise that corporations are competing for talent in an increasing situation of scarcity (as demonstrated above), then very few companies should be able to attract *only* top talent. Any large organisation will have a distribution of high-, medium- and low-performing leaders. If these leaders are drawn from a single talent pool (e.g. men), there will be less choice than if drawing from two pools (both sexes). A company with a richer gender mix will end up with more of the 'head' of the distribution (high performers) and less of the 'tail' (low performers).

One can model, for a specific organisation, the impact of having a higher proportion of high performers and compare it with the cost of creating this higher gender mix. In our work for UK-based large professional services firms we established for example that a gender-rich partnership (50 per cent women) would have an 11 per cent greater gross revenue per partner than an all-male one, as illustrated in Figure 2.4. The number doubles to 20 per cent when taking into consideration the leverage effect: successful partners tend to 'feed' more junior staff than unsuccessful ones. This translates into a profit differential for *all* partners of tens of thousands of pounds each year, an amount well in excess of the cash costs linked to facilitating greater gender diversity.

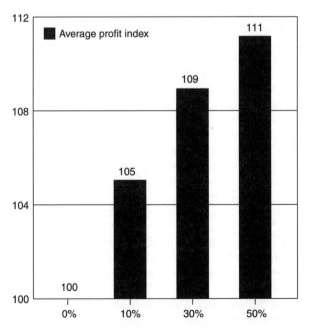

Figure 2.4 **Impact of percentage of women partners on per partner profits**

A professional services firm is relatively easy to model, but we argue that pretty much every business can create a reasonable proxy measure of cash performance by looking at areas where they have high versus low performers. We would strongly encourage readers to do so as this helps create extremely robust business cases for gender-related spend, including coaching: everybody benefits financially from a shift in gender balance at the top.

Corporate examples

There have been many studies of overall gender diversity and corporate performance. For instance a Swedish study of 14,000 companies (Swedish Business Development Agency, 1999) demonstrated a very strong correlation between gender representation and all four key performance measures of productivity, net value added, net profitability and return on total capital.

Studies demonstrating the impact of diversity at the top of corporations have started to emerge too: often quoted is Roy Adler's (Adler, 2001) research of Fortune 500 businesses between 1980 and 1998. This was probably the first study that had both a good sample size (215 large companies) and longitudinal data over a fairly long period. Adler used a point system depending on how many women were part of the top 10 management team and were part of the Board. He rewarded 'pioneering companies' by allocating more points in the early years than in subsequent periods. He chose three financial measures and compared the companies' performance with the median of their respective industries. The results showed a clear pattern: Fortune 500 firms with a high number of women executives outperformed their industry median firms on all financial measures. Furthermore, the firms with the very best scores for promoting women were consistently more profitable than those whose scores were merely very good, as shown in Table 2.1.

The data have been added to every subsequent year with similar results. In 2008, the researchers decided to take a new angle and plot 'the 100 most desirable MBA employers for women' (compiled by *Fortune* magazine). Although the

Table 2.1 Financial performance and gender diversity

Measure	Gender-diverse management	25 companies median performance	Performance difference
Profits/revenues	6.4%	4.8%	+34%
Profits/assets	6.5%	5.5%	+18%
Profits/share-holders' equity	26.5%	15.7%	+69%

list had to be whittled down to 56 to fit the criteria of the rest of the data, the results were pretty much the same: 55 per cent of companies had profits higher than the median for example. Although Adler recognises that correlation doesn't prove causation, he argues that the consistency of results over time is impressive and calculates that the odds of all measures coming out on the side favouring women on a random basis are 262,114 to 1.

Another interesting academic study over a long period (1992–2006) was carried out at Columbia University (Dezso and Ross, 2008) and measured the 'female impact' on company market value (using Tobin's Q – a widely used financial ratio). Interestingly, the study of 1,500 organisations found a positive association between company performance and female participation below the CEO level, but no positive effects from having a female CEO. Specifically, the authors show that the performance differential is particularly large in firms pursuing an 'innovation-intensive' strategy, where creativity and collaboration may be especially important.

Even more recently, McKinsey looked at the direct and indirect financial performance of gender-rich organisations (Desvaux, Devillard-Hoellinger and Meaney, 2008): they studied over 230 organisations representing 115,000 employees and drew two interesting conclusions:

- Companies with three women or more in their top management teams scored systematically higher in nine organisational dimensions. They asked over 58,000 employees to rate their company in terms of capability, leadership, motivation, innovation, work environment, etc. Some of the differences were small but gender-rich organisations outscored others every single time. Interestingly, 92 of the Fortune 500 companies have three women on their boards, but this is highly biased towards fashion and retail. Another study of the top 500 Australian companies (excluding mining) shows that, although 37 per cent have women on their boards, only 2 per cent have at least three – this is in keeping with our observations of hundreds of corporate clients.

- Companies which did score higher in all nine dimensions (top quartile) had a systematically higher financial performance than their peers: an operational profitability that was 68 per cent above the group average (measured by EBITDA); and a market value 62 per cent above the group average (measured as enterprise value/book value).

If you dig even deeper into the research, you find a small number of inconclusive studies where other factors are too entangled to enable the gender impact to come out strongly. However not a single study advocates that women-rich management teams have a lower performance than traditional ones. So the conclusion should be fairly obvious, given that:

- corporations need to engage and retain more women leaders to fill the depleting ranks of (mostly male) Baby Boomers;
- a clear mathematical business case can be made to advocate a more balanced leadership team; and
- most studies demonstrate a strong positive correlation between a high female participation in the management team and financial performance.

Twenty-first century organisations must take urgent action to increase the number of women in their senior ranks. A key milestone will be to achieve the participation of at least three women in the top team (management steering committee, executive director or non-executive chairman). Obviously, this is not an overnight process: we must first understand what drives the dramatic fallout from 60+ per cent of graduates to but a handful of women on executive boards around the world.

Managing the Leadership Pipeline

'We haven't had a lot of failures in senior women. We know that once we give them the jobs they do pretty well. We just haven't been giving them the jobs.'

Sandy Ogg, Unilever Global Head of HR discussing what his company is doing to improve the women's leadership pipeline.

If even a company as sophisticated as Unilever recognises that their proportion of senior female managers drops from 50 per cent in front-line management to 6 per cent at senior executive level, we know that the Leadership Pipeline and its associated drop-off points need active management. In Chapter 3 we discuss in detail the coaching needs of women at various stages of their careers; here we simply look at the financial impact of haemorrhaging talent.

The business case will vary tremendously from company to company but the idea is to compare two 'departure curves' as illustrated in Figure 2.5. The first curve represents the typical female attrition in a global corporation at various career stages. This is the net number of women employed from an initial group of 50 per cent women/50 per cent men, all the way to the 5 per cent women/95 per cent men at a very senior level. These of course are percentages: they need to be correlated to the absolute number of people at each career stage. It is also worth noting that this is based on career-stage measures and it doesn't track specific cohorts; the actual number of women from a given group is likely to be much less than 5 per cent by the time one gets to senior management due to replacement/recruitment.

Against this first departure curve, one can plot a 'gender-neutral' departure curve, i.e. the normal attrition that represents the ebb and flow of employment at a given company. This is typically expressed by the formula:

$$N_t = N_0(1 - i)^t,$$

where N_0 is the starting number of staff, i is the proportion of staff leaving each year and t is the number of years. The formula can be refined by estimating the proportion of

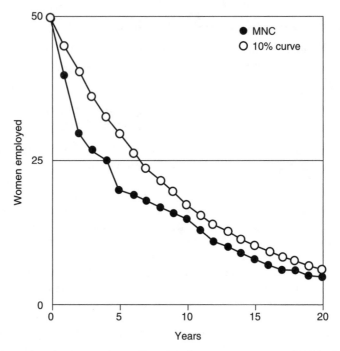

Figure 2.5 Women attrition in a global corporation v. standard 10 per cent attrition

women who were hired to replace a departing woman. The second line in Figure 2.5 represents a typical 10 per cent net attrition rate over 20 years. Again, one needs to compare oranges with oranges: i.e. absolute numbers with absolute numbers, percentages with percentages, cohorts with cohorts.

The difference between the two lines gives the scope of intervention, i.e. where we need to invest in order to get closer to the natural attrition curve. This obviously includes investing in coaching. It then becomes relatively straightforward to build a specific business case, using measures such as the cost of recruiting/training versus the cost of coaching and other interventions.

It is now time to dig deeper into what makes women

leave at various stages in their career and how coaching can help. That is the object of Chapter 3.

Implications when Coaching Women to Lead

- As companies compete for emerging leadership talent, women represent an under-used resource. Coaching has a critical role to play in retaining a critical mass of women in the corporation's talent pool.
- The evidence of female success at senior levels should be used in coaching to increase the confidence of aspiring women leaders as well as that of the mostly male incumbents to give them their rightful place.
- It is the responsibility of HR professionals and sponsoring executives to develop robust business cases for coaching using one or several of the arguments above.

What are the critical stages of a woman's career and their coaching requirements?

On the 16th December 2003, the top BBC news item announced (BBC News, 2003): 'women have overtaken men at every level of education in developed countries around the world, and girls are now more confident of getting better-paid, professional jobs than their flagging male counterparts'. It went on to say that in the UK, 63 per cent of girls expected to have 'white collar, high-skilled' jobs by the time they were 30 compared to only 51 per cent of boys. In the early to mid 1990s, most multinationals, professional firms and FTSE 100 companies were taking on at least 50 per cent women at graduate entry level – simply because academically, psychometrically, in social skills and life-skill tests they were the best of the crop. Today, taking on *more* than 50 per cent women at this level (and other levels) is becoming common practice for many companies and professional firms.

This proportion of qualified women in the workplace comfortably exceeds the national average as seen in Figure 3.1: women represent about 45 per cent of the labour force all the way to age 50. So why do women only occupy just 5 per cent of the seats around UK board tables? [The proportion in listed companies (FTSE 250) is 7.3 per cent according to Cranfield School of Management (Sealy, Vinnicombe and Doldor, with De Anca and Hoel, 2009) but actually decreases steadily with company size. A typical figure of 5 per cent nationwide is more representative.] To understand this, we need to look at the different stages of a woman's career and find out what happens along the way.

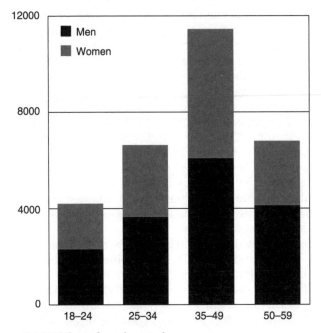

Figure 3.1 UK labour force by gender

Level 1 – starting out (from age 22)

Women enter the workforce with a high confidence level after graduating at approximately 22. They are usually in their first job because they are the best: they have the highest academic grades and have passed various interview processes with flying colours to land the job.

In their first role, there is bound to be a level of learning, whether it is professional exams (accountants, lawyers, doctors), managerial training or gaining experience on the job. Again, statistics show women do well at this level. There are other factors at work here as well. Most young women at this stage are focused on their job and are doing well – they want to go for promotion, learn all they can quickly, because for many they are already aware their focus may change in a few years' time.

A new layer of complexity emerges, however: the job gets a bit tougher and it is no longer just about getting accurate results. The parallel with simple academic success starts to diverge. This is all about coaching and adapting to change with some calculated risk-taking. For instance, women need to find their way through the labyrinth of career progression. This labyrinth takes on many shapes and paths and it is not until a woman understands the unwritten rules driven by company culture that she will discover what type of career path takes her to the next level.

It is unlikely that a company would invest in coaching at such a junior level, so this is where well-trained managers can play an invaluable role as both coaches (helping her find her own path) and mentors (knowledge of the unwritten rules and networks).

In the first instance, it is important to remind women of the hopes and generally high self-esteem they have at this stage combined with an optimism concerning what lies ahead. Taking them back to how good they felt on their first day at work, and helping them remember all their hopes and dreams about what they felt they could achieve, perhaps after a great training course for example, can prove helpful.

Also, until women map out the territory, they cannot make informed choices – the manager can alternate between mentor and coach to support this process. This can be supplemented by networks targeted at junior women managers, especially when these include contact with more senior women in the company who are genuine role models.

Level 2 – assistant/junior manager (age 24–26)

At this point women are still generally career-oriented and pushing on. However, often internally, this is when they begin to ask significant questions about their careers. Questions such as:

- Do I compete or not to move on in my job?
- Do I decide to act like a woman at work, or to mimic a man's way of working to get on?
- Or do I become a Queen Bee type? This is the woman who,

despite her powerful position, needs to be the centre of attention at all times and regards other women as threats to her ability to enjoy exclusive attention and respect. Margaret Thatcher was a Queen Bee type.

These are essential questions around a woman finding her identity at work and deciding how to act accordingly. Note that men rarely go through the same process of 'Who shall I be at work today?', 'How shall I act/do my job?' and 'How shall I manage my colleagues?'

Choosing role models – or not – is very important for women. This is partly because senior female role models are few and far between, but also they are not necessarily appealing. Margaret Thatcher, Rebekah Wade (Chief Executive of News International) and Carly Fiorina (former CEO of Hewlett Packard) may have done very well in their careers but not everybody wants to act like them at work. For many, however, successful alternative role models are few and far between. Identifying role models inside and outside of the workplace, analysing what makes them special, then turning those qualities into personal actions can be very helpful for women at this stage of their careers.

It goes deeper. One of the major issues a woman has these days is fulfilling all the roles she has thrust on her by society: whether it is heavy-socialising singleton; perfect partner; domestic goddess; arch entertainer as well as aiming to continuously look good (perfect hair, skin, nails and well dressed) – and that is all additional to being a successful career woman.

Identity – and working identity – is key to coaching at this stage. This is the level where women often need to give themselves permission to be authentic to themselves. This is when women will need to discover their own personal style, feel good about it and develop a management style that reflects their personality in an effort to be true to themselves. Our experience demonstrates clearly that it is at this stage when women really start to need help with self-esteem to be able to bring their whole selves to the workplace.

Beyond this, women need to be able to understand the company culture and what it takes to be successful within that organisation. Generally speaking, men at this stage find it much easier to understand the code to success at work. This is possibly because those codes are set by men – male boards of directors over the decades, sometimes even centuries – in the first place. From a coaching point of view, women may need extra time and help to break the code and work out how they can not only be successful but can make it work well for them – there are plenty of successful women in senior roles who are unhappy on a daily basis. If women do not find this particular balance, it is more than likely they will eventually leave the organisation.

By the end of the combined periods of Levels 1 and 2, many women have already dropped out, despite the initial optimism and drive to do well. Typically 15–20 per cent of our initial 50 per cent have left: we are already considerably below the national labour averages. Some have entered long-term relationships just as they were leaving university and wish to start a family early. Others decide that the 'corporate thing' is not for them and pursue alternative careers or set up their own business. Although it may seem that there is little that companies can do at this stage to retrieve the situation, managing this outflow is critical: unless companies can get a solid 30 per cent female population into middle management, they will not be able to create a robust enough pipeline all the way to the Board, with consequences detailed in Chapter 2.

Coaching at this stage is likely to be seen as expensive yet it is a worthwhile investment, especially when revisiting the shape of the departure curves in Figure 2.5 in Chapter 2. A blended programme including networking with role models, group coaching and limited one-to-one input is likely to be the best mix. This is why so many pro-active women's networks are being developed in large professional services firms, international banks and consumer goods companies, among others. In fact the largest graduate recruiters are those with the largest investment at risk when their young managers drop out. Programmes should also strive to re-engage leavers. Building a women-friendly corporation (see Chapter 8) and the judicious investment in coaching as part of a talent strategy will help with retention.

Level 3 – middle-manager (age 27–30)

On reaching this stage, she is clear about what she wants. Her attitude: 'Who cares, I'm doing the job anyway' launches her forward. This is also the stage when it starts to go wrong for women. It is traditionally when companies stop listening and stop caring about their 'best and brightest graduate recruits'. Until recently, most companies and professional firms have been in denial about the differences between men and women at work. They assume that we are all human beings and that we should be treated the same.

This is also true of coaches. Until recently, business coaching in the UK has tended to think and act along the same lines. As coaches, the usual response is that we would always view clients from the same starting point. However, given the differences between men and women at work, their different needs and the glaring inequalities in the workplace (half who join are women, just 5 per cent of board directors are women), we do need to think and coach differently if we are ever going to help women achieve happiness and equality in the workplace.

If a woman has not already joined a women's network in the workplace (either internally or externally) by this stage, she should strongly think about doing so. However, there are networks and networks. The type where often too many consultants are trying to sell to a few corporate members, or to each other, do not give women's networks (or any other) a good name. Corporate in-house networks which are set up to help retain and promote good women are useful, as are external ones which are informative and full of other like-minded women – whether it is to ask each other for professional mentoring advice or to swap stories about children. Coaching can be invaluable when it helps women focus on understanding network dynamics, grasping strong and loose affiliation.

The child-bearing years

The average age for women in the UK to have their first child is 29. This is when their career vision begins to appear in a different context. Before children, most women see life in the context of work – and after the first baby, it is work in the context of life. There is no doubt about it that carrying a baby, giving birth and becoming a mother gives most women a different vision of their world, which in turn gives them a different meaning and purpose to their work. Just ask yourself, how many mothers do you hear at work say (or privately admit) 'I'd rather be at home with my baby/kids'? Whether that really is the case, and there is plenty of research to suggest that while most working mothers return to work because they want to, having children fundamentally changes the way women view their work. It also changes the way in which they work. Many working mothers choose to return to the workplace part-time (the UK has one of the largest numbers of women part-time workers in the world – see Chapter 9) which, whether they like it or not, immediately places them a step further away from more senior jobs.

Focus also changes. More women at this stage are task-focused (usually to get the day job done before they return home to the night job of caring for their families). While there are plenty of studies to suggest women are extremely focused and productive in this mode, there is also evidence to suggest that they tend to skip vital areas to career progression such as networking, being political at work and also creating vision in the workplace.

The first 100 days back at work after maternity leave are almost as important to women as the first 100 days for a new CEO. As a senior gender diversity practitioner (and mother of three) said recently, 'most women have to prove they didn't throw out their brains with the placenta!' There have been plenty of studies – both academic and lifestyle – that show the biggest single issue women face when they return to work after maternity leave is speaking the business language. This works on several levels: if a woman has spent six months mainly at home with her baby she will be immersed in baby-talk, but at a more subtle level it is also important to read and remember the nuances of business language used at work.

This is also a major stage in her career when a woman is likely to leave her job – not just in the UK, but globally. This is such an important decision because evidence suggests that if a woman leaves the workforce at this stage she will find it extremely hard to re-enter. If she does, she will never catch up with peers who remained in the role either in seniority or pay. In a typical multinational, another 10 per cent will leave at this stage, meaning there are 20–25 per cent women left. We can already see, it is becoming critical for companies because they are now below their 30 per cent women managers talent pipeline.

'Superwoman', mother of six and investment fund owner Nicola Horlick taking part in a live Q&A on *The Guardian* website in April 2008, in response to a question on post-maternity return to work, said: 'I think this is one of the biggest challenges facing our country. Getting well-educated women back into the workforce after a career break must be a priority. It is a shameful waste of resource to discard these women.'

Coaching around maternity issues

Coaching around maternity is already a big business area, and other than leadership coaching, it is probably the most sought-after coaching by companies for women in the workplace.

Given the above, there are several key areas coaches need to address. Confidence and self-esteem is a huge need at this point – both in everyday life and at work – because having a baby is a life-changing event. Given bonding time, lack of sleep and the general change in the woman's routine, let alone her body, during maternity leave – it is not difficult to understand what a challenge it can be returning to the workplace.

There are external, practical aspects about returning to work over which mothers often need re-assurance, from childcare to working hours and discussions with line managers about what the team has been working on while they have been on maternity leave. Building confidence helps women to structure more difficult conversations around their return, including discussions with partners and managers.

There are also important issues around inclusion. It is

easy not to feel part of a team on returning to work. While the team should work to include members, it is also up to the woman herself to make herself included. Again, various coaching approaches can help.

If women haven't done so already before, joining networks at this stage, both inside and outside the company, can help enormously. Spending a lunch hour discussing returning to work and babies with others in a similar situation and with those who have been through the experience can be reassuring and informative.

Managing emotion in the workplace is often important at this stage. Many women claim to be far more emotional once they have had a baby and, while this can be a good thing overall – the best leaders demonstrate high emotional intelligence (EI) – excessive emotion in the workplace does not help women get on. Looking at the benefits that EI can bring to a management role is as important as considering why 'over-emoting' or losing it emotionally at work is unhelpful. A scenario-based coaching session with reminders of good practice focusing on how to handle situations using a high level of emotional competence can be useful.

Finally, if after coaching, a woman decides she really does want to leave the workplace to become a full-time mother, it should be because she wants to do this and not, as is often the case, 'OK I'll just be a Mum'. It should be a well thought out and positive decision, not a poor compromise.

Level 4 – senior manager (age 32–35)

This is the stage where there are now noticeably fewer women – approximately 10 per cent of the original 50 per cent who joined at graduate level. If you are a woman wanting to progress to this stage, you will be competing mostly against men and there will be very few female role models or mentors for women to benchmark with and gain inside help and information.

Traditionally, women have issues deciding whether or not to go for the next job. Coaching around such decisions can be vital. From a company's point of view, it wants women to demonstrate they are ready to go for the job, not deliberating on it. To get to this point women have to be really sure they want the job – far more so than men. It comes back to confidence. There is a saying in the corporate world that 'a man will look at a job description and if he can do 30 per cent of it will apply for the job; a woman will see that she can do 70 per cent of it and think she is not eligible to apply'.

A helpful approach here is for the woman to apply for the job anyway, i.e. make a decision to go through the application and interview process, and then decide later if offered the job whether she wants to take it. If women never take up the challenge of senior roles, the message they are sending out is that they are not interested, rather than being partly interested or even very interested but not sure they have the capabilities. Coaching that can make a difference will include encouraging women to stretch themselves, to look at closed mindsets and beliefs about ability, to improve decision making and the confidence that they are well qualified and highly thought of enough to be able to apply for the job.

It is also extremely important that women acknowledge their whole selves, including their inner selves at this point. What does it take for a woman to go for a senior role? Other than inherent capability it is also perspective. Talking with women at this stage they will refer to 'a need to do something more challenging', 'a hunger inside that needs satisfying' or 'there's more to me than this'. However, a lot of women shut it down because they balance it out with other aspects to their lives such as children or caring roles.

Men, on the other hand, nearly always express 'their inner hunger' and 'need to be more challenged' in the corporate arena because they can still express it best there – it remains the natural place for them to grow, but this is not traditionally so for women. Women need to knock on closed doors, search for different keys until they get the right one and then move around a labyrinth to find a way forward. For men, the door is open if they want to enter when they knock, and any progress they make is generally based on a straightforward linear line.

Stretch jobs

Often in the past, what is known as a 'stretch job' – a short-term assignment up to a year or so in which managers must prove themselves – is a way up the career ladder. Typically these challenging roles would mean reorganising a problematic business or setting up a new office in a different location for example. Since the recession this has changed a little in that less of these roles are available. This could help women overall because this is traditionally a tipping point at which most women will refuse to take on such a role.

If they do need to go for it, however, it is very important that women (or men for the same reason) believe they can change and turn around the situation to do a great job. The difference for women is often knowing what is required to deliver the results – having to figure out the internal, cultural success measures as well as what appears on paper as the business delivery goals. Again, this is something most men do not seem to battle with: they believe they know instantly what is required.

Coaching help may concentrate on checking motivation for this new role, brainstorming the impact of this change on their lives, building confidence in their ability to perform, contemplating a range of problem-solving and decision-making approaches and testing their strategic thinking.

Finally, if they take on such a role women need to be very clear about why they have taken it on. Is it to further their career? To be paid extra for a year? And to look at those facts with all the hopes and limitations they place on the individual, but particularly a woman with all the extra roles she may have (mother, carer, partner, best friend, glamorous businesswoman, domestic goddess, etc.).

Level 5 – the Board

The UK has just 5 per cent of female board directors currently, a figure that has gone down slightly in the last few years – it also represents a tiny percentage of the original 50 per cent who started out in the workplace. There will be only a handful of women available who are qualified, have the relevant experience and the guts to take on a board role.

Before they start, or even apply for the role, women need to go through a massive scoping exercise to really understand what they are taking on. There is the content: What is the role all about? And there is the context: What am I getting into? Who are the other players? What is my contribution? How will mine be different to theirs? Where am I going ultimately? Where are they going? And what does winning mean and look like? In many ways these are straight leadership questions, which either gender applying for a board role may ask themselves. But this is also the stage at which most women fail.

In this arena, women often respond with excessive humility, or more occasionally the opposite – excessive arrogance. This may be partly because they don't know how to respond, or more likely that, because of the extraordinary and tough situation they find themselves in, they are unable to be themselves, to be comfortable in their own skin.

Coaching at this stage should be a constant reminder as to why women are at this point. Is it just because they are extremely good at what they do? Key questions at this time could include: How do I contribute? Which unique things do I bring to this board table that will move the business forward? As a result of the current economic situation, the emphasis is currently on delivery, and providing directors can deliver they will survive.

But what other unique features do women bring to the board table? A recent survey by US diversity agency Catalyst of the Fortune Top 500 companies showed that those which performed best (including bottom line) were those with more women and more women at very senior levels. Further, in the recently published McKinsey & Company's *Women Matter 2* (2008) it shows that senior women globally are more likely to develop the leadership qualities to reinforce the competitive edge in companies' finance and organisation than men do. Closing the gender gap on decision making increases business competitiveness.

There is also a very real argument for saying the recent financial crisis would not have been as dramatic as it has been if there had been more women in senior positions in stock exchanges, banks and financial institutions. Experts have noted that without women at senior decision-making levels there is a lack of balance and moderation (women are noted for being strong on good governance) that gender equality brings. There is also a lack of creativity in finding expert solutions – simply because different views (those of women and others) are ignored. If the typical board of a bank is made up of white, middle-aged men it stands to reason you will get similar views and solutions. Further, that they lack creativity to push the business on, or come up with new, radical solutions has not helped banks either.

Coaching women directors

So what are the special coaching requirements of women leaders?

We are continuously refining our thinking through our research and experience with clients and have come to the conclusion that you must both develop leaders and give them the tools to do their job. The tools can be of a strategic nature, of a team-building nature or simply to cover areas that are new to the leader. For balanced leadership we would argue these include visibility, resilience, being strategic, EI, making decisions, acting intellectually, behaving as a leader and being a meaningful leader.

Of these leadership skills and behaviours, probably the most important to women right now include being strategic, developing vision skills and building confidence and self-esteem.

Becoming a strategic thinker is a journey that means changing one's outlook about the nature of business as well as confidence-boosting experiences. A good coach can accelerate both the decision making around specific issues and the maturity of thinking strategically about an industry or a business unit. Additionally, senior women may choose to acquire specialist knowledge in certain areas of strategic analysis that is particularly relevant to their role or industry. This ranges from scenario planning to business modelling or strategic valuation.

Developing vision for many women has been an issue for some time as the *Harvard Business Review* commented in the article, 'Women and the vision thing', January 2009 (Ibarra and Obodaru, 2009). Not only does lack of vision make constant appearances in women's appraisals, but it can hold women back when going for top roles. There are many reasons given why women seem less likely to develop vision at work than men: they tend to be more task-based, and often display vision elsewhere, in the community for example. However, it is important that they develop vision and use it at work to get on. Coaching for this can stem from building a very personal vision (creating a vision board, mind-mapping, etc.) to extending these techniques to create a vision for a department, or team or a company-wide vision for the workplace.

Resilience is another area that senior women often want help with. Modern business leaders continually travel, often eat the wrong things at the wrong time and often accumulate a sleep deficit. They drive themselves hard, drawing on outstanding mental and physical stamina. This can come at an unaffordable cost to the individual, family and business. Assessing clients on sleep patterns and habits, nutrition, exercise routines and stamina, hydration, as well as other health and stress measures is the best way forward.

To deal with emotional/psychological resilience is just as important. We all know senior people who 'lose it' when faced with difficulties, either withdrawing, becoming sullen and moody, or who respond with aggression and anger, often shouting at people, taking their frustration out on others and a myriad of other nonproductive and unhelpful emotionally driven reactions. Even those who don't react to difficulties, ambiguity and hard problems in such extreme ways often find themselves at the mercy of their emotions, for example, making poor decisions, misdiagnosing problems, creating weak solutions or just being stressed. Using positive psychology, coupled with exercise and a good eating plan can make all the difference.

Work–life balance may also play a part for senior women, particularly if they have families and are working long hours. Some honest assessments around work–life balance, accompanied by challenging mindsets (e.g. Do you always need to work late? Can you influence a long-hours culture? Is there an evening a week you could leave early?) can help as can making and practising behaviour changes. Dealing with mind, body and behaviour, and creating a personalised programme that takes into account the demands and schedule of the individual is important. It is also good to remember that mentally and physically honed leaders function better for longer at the peak of their game.

Other than this, coaching around confidence and self-esteem remains vital for most women, no matter how senior they are. There are plenty of coaching methods, tools and interventions for coaching in this area. Confidence is more external, something individuals can put on and is subject to other people's views. Some of the tools we have found that have worked best for self-esteem include cultivating self-appreciation by counting three 'blessings' or good things that went well each day before going to sleep and looking at 'self-talk' or the way in which individuals talk to themselves.

When women have worked on confidence and self-esteem, the outcomes are manifest. For a start they think differently from those who suffer from a lack of confidence and low self-esteem. They will always speak out at meetings and be heard. They don't automatically back down when challenged and they make sure that no matter what everyone else has said, they still have something to say. Beyond that they give themselves respect. Confident women don't wait for everyone else to tell them how good they are, they have their own means for strengthening their self-respect. They know what their strengths are, they know what they do well and they know how to give and gain respect. Another area in which they gain is by networking and knowing how to network successfully. They have lots of ways of meeting and greeting people, they know how to initiate contact with people and they know how to talk to people. Finally, confident women can protect their own boundaries. They can stand their ground, explain themselves and manage difficult people whether it's their bosses or difficult customers. They have ways of explaining themselves clearly, of accounting for their decisions, of handling negativity with gravitas.

Conclusion

These stages of a woman's career provide a guideline to coaches. They are not written in stone, but follow the pattern of most leading larger and mid-sized companies in the UK and often internationally. Understanding and reviewing the critical stages of a woman's career is fundamental to coaching women, particularly senior women, or those on the talent trail. Without this understanding, coaches are armed with fewer tools for the job. Knowing what is required at different stages, what women may be going through early on in their career, or what they may need when they join the boardroom are equally as important. More specific examples of coaching approaches and techniques are outlined in Chapter 6.

Implications when Coaching Women to Lead

- Women's needs vary at different career and life stages.
- The key stage when it can go wrong is Level 3 (middle manager – age 27–30) – and this is when a lot of women cut their careers short, and when companies lose their investment/a valuable part of their executive pipeline.
- Early confidence and optimism should be maintained or re-ignited.
- Coaching needs to bridge home, personal and professional life to be successful.
- Coaches should be conscious of the complexity of the labyrinth and that women's path may not be straight.

What do women want? Reporting the results of our research

Before we define specific interventions for Coaching Women to Lead, we need to validate which areas and domains will give women the best results for a given level of investment – time, money and organisational effort. We knew we had good insight into what women wanted from our client work, but felt that this needed to be supplemented by objective research, both quantitative and qualitative. This chapter is the first of two where we report research findings. It is based on a survey jointly designed with a post-graduate student at the London School of Economics and Political Science (LSE) for an MSc in Organisational and Social Psychology (Walvoort, 2009). Chapter 5 follows and reports back on interviews with senior women/potential role models.

Research context and design

Janna Walvoort of the LSE, identified – through an extensive literature review – the main barriers to women's advancement in organisations and eight separate coping strategies thought to be commonly used to overcome these barriers. These strategies are:

- family and career balance
- understanding corporate culture
- systematic investment in career and development
- confidence
- knowledge of own strengths
- networking

- role models
- career planning.

Janna then worked with Averil Leimon of White Water Strategies (WWS) to develop a questionnaire (Appendix 1) to test these coping strategies with women currently in a corporate role. Research objectives included testing whether these strategies were the correct ones, if any of them stood out, and if specific insight could be gleaned on how to implement these strategies. Additional objectives specific to this book included determining in which circumstances or in which areas of intervention coaching would be most appropriate.

The questionnaire combined quantitative and qualitative methods, using both closed and open questions, and was completed online. Respondents were drawn from an executive database, a business women's network as well as interviewees from Chapter 5. In turn, each woman was asked to pass the research link on to others. The questionnaire was completed in confidence.

Questions asked

The full questionnaire can be found in Appendix 1. Below is a summary.

The online survey commenced with the usual filtering and demographic questions. The main quantitative approach was to ask respondents to distribute 100 points between each of the eight strategies listed above using three filters:

1. What helped their career in the past?
2. What would have helped?
3. What would help now?

This quantification allowed us to carry out some variance analysis and other statistical tests to validate research hypotheses.

The qualitative aspects of the survey investigated:

- What would make women more likely to become tomorrow's leaders?

- What is or was the biggest challenge in building their career?
- What advice would they give a younger woman who is at the start of her career?

Demographics and level of information

A total of 125 women responded to the survey. The 107 who were currently working in a corporate environment were asked specific quantitative questions relating to their corporate experience. All 125 responses were used for analysis of the open questions.

The majority worked full-time, with only six women working part-time. Their professional experience ranged from 1 to 35 years with a mean of 16.5 years: 0–10 years of experience ($n = 35$); 11–20 years of experience ($n = 36$); more than 20 years of experience ($n = 36$). This correlated broadly with their self-reported career stages: 21 were at junior-level management; 31 were at middle-level management; 55 were at senior-level management.

Respondents were drawn from a wide range of industries as illustrated in Figure 4.1, although one could argue that manufacturing is probably under-represented. Further research could include replicating this survey but controlling

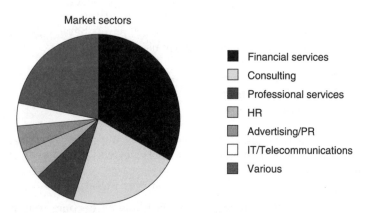

Market sectors

- Financial services
- Consulting
- Professional services
- HR
- Advertising/PR
- IT/Telecommunications
- Various

Figure 4.1 Distribution of respondents by industry

for a more representative sample of the management population (UK or otherwise).

Finally, respondents followed a normal (bell-shaped) distribution when asked about how well informed they were when they had to make big career decisions: most were neither in the dark nor in full possession of the facts.

Primary findings

The following key results were statistically significant:

- All eight strategies are important at all career stages.
- Four strategies stand out as particularly helpful when looking at what has helped in the past.
- Support from senior women is essential to increase the number of women leaders.

Qualitative answers also provide insight on *how* to develop and implement these coping strategies: which type of networking, how to boost confidence, how to use strengths, etc.

Finally, qualitative data identified two further potential coping strategies: *work ethics* and *gender behaviour*. Let us examine these results in greater detail.

All eight strategies are important at all career stages

Figure 4.2 shows the relative strength of each coping strategy, combining all relevant quantitative questions (the chart shows the confidence intervals for each variable). In the first analysis *networking* overlaps with *confidence*. *Role models* also scores highly. Secondary analysis (paired samples *t*-tests, with added analysis to account for the codependence between variables) shows that networking edges ahead as the most important strategy and there is no one strategy that can be rejected as not being significant. The analysis holds true when looking at the three questions separately.

For readers who want to explore results a bit deeper, we present the raw results for each of the three related quantitative questions in Appendix 1 (Tables A1 to A3 and graphic representations of the main answers in Figures A1–A5).

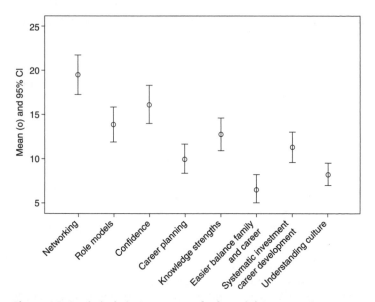

Figure 4.2 **Statistical importance of the eight strategies: mean distribution of 100 points and 95% confidence interval**

As networking stands out, it is important to distinguish between typical male networking (e.g. of a commercial nature) and the type of networking sought by women in the survey. As seen in qualitative answers, this is very much networking for mutual support and understanding the rules of the game, as well as meeting more senior people. There were hardly any references to external networks in the qualitative answers. This is perfectly aligned with the barriers to women's advancement described in the literature review carried out in Janna's research; i.e. even today the unwritten rules of performance and behaviour are largely dictated by a white male heritage. It also has important implications in terms of both coaching and organisational support as we shall see below.

We expected the use of the strategies to differ depending on the level of experience of respondents. It is interesting to learn that increasing *confidence* for example remains a valid theme throughout women's careers. This is certainly consistent with the interviews in Chapter 5 and has implications for coaching.

Only *career planning* was statistically distinct when compared across age/experience groups. As expected, there was a statistical difference between the oldest age group and the younger ones. There is also a difference when looking at the question *would have helped in the past*. In other words, women suggest that, with hindsight, they should have paid more attention to career management, or planning, than they have. There are many possible reasons for this from carefree youth, to a focus on doing the job right early in a career, to delaying big career decisions until after children. Again, the interviews in Chapter 5 shed an interesting light on these questions.

Four strategies stand out as particularly helpful

When looking at the scores in the Appendix tables (A1–A3), it is interesting to note that the scores for each strategy look very different, even if they are all important. We therefore carried out further analysis to check if there were any *clusters* – statistical groupings between strategies. The answer varies depending on which of the three questions you analyse. The most interesting cluster is that, in response to the question *What HAS helped in the past?* A clear cluster emerges containing the following four strategies:

- networking
- role models
- confidence
- knowledge of strengths.

What is also interesting is that, in response to the same question, all other strategies score low; i.e. they have not helped much, and there is no middle-scoring cluster.

For the other two questions, although there are some clusters, they tend to be quite broad and towards the middle values; i.e. they don't tell us much.

Support from senior women is essential to increase the number of women leaders

When asked, *Which of the following do you think would make women more likely to become tomorrow's leaders?*, support from senior women came out loud and clear, as illustrated in Figure 4.3.

Affirmative action was lower, even when adding general affirmative action to board quotas. There was, however, an interesting spread of recommendations in the *Other* category. Advice was dispensed along three main themes.

Support

This theme included already mentioned themes of support networks, mentoring and fair processes. Interestingly, 10 per cent of respondents spontaneously asked for support from

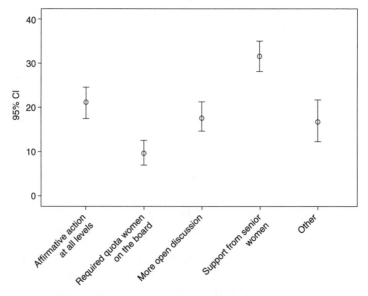

What would make women more likely to become tomorrow's leaders?

Figure 4.3 **Factors that would make women more likely to become leaders: Mean distribution of 100 points and 95% confidence interval**

senior men, some suggesting men/women reverse mentoring – a theme we cover in Chapter 8.

Work–life balance (WLB)

About 20 per cent of respondents made concrete suggestions to improve WLB. This is particularly interesting in light of the relatively low score of WLB as a coping strategy as seen above. Is it because most policies are already in place in large organisations? Is it because it is a 'lost cause' – i.e. women know it is essential but they think asking for it will single them out as troublemakers? We do not have the answer but this contrast is worrying.

Changing culture and mentality

Many interesting suggestions, which were not limited to women in organisations, emerged in this section. For example, respondents clearly thought that younger women entering the workforce must be agents of change.

Many examples and two further strategies

The questionnaire finished with two big open questions:

- What do you think is or was the biggest challenge in building your career?
- What advice would you give a younger woman who is at the start of her career?

The answers were used in two ways:

- as an illustration of the pre-established eight strategies;
- as a source of further strategies.

The answers were then regrouped as themes until a pattern emerged.

The biggest challenge

Women were challenged in five areas as illustrated in Table 4.1 below. These reinforce the quantitative data and provide specific themes for coaching.

Table 4.1 Grouped themes and examples – the biggest challenge

Theme	Example quotes
Career progression	
Lack of career planning	'No career strategy and lack of understanding about why it is important' 'Once I realised the importance of . . . career planning, I was able to move more quickly through the organisation'
Lack of direction	'Figuring out where I wanted to go'
Lack of education	'My own lack of understanding of how learning new skills is extremely worthwhile'
Confidence	
Lack of self-belief	'My own lack of belief that I could become a senior leader' 'Overcoming my own insecurities and inadequacies'
Others' expectations	'Knowing when to say No' 'Learning to deal with always available "always on" expectation from corporations'
Organisational dynamics	
Lack of understanding culture	'Developing sufficient understanding of working culture to understand how to make it work for me'
Lack of understanding politics	'Knowing how and when it is socially acceptable to offer opinions' 'Finding out the "rules of the game" – the informal way things work and the ways others play the game to their advantage' 'Understanding the politics of the office'
Relational support	
Lack of networking	'Understanding the importance of building and using networks' Women can be excluded from the golf course [. . .] and informal one-to-one relationship building sessions in male-dominated environments. 'Not enough networking while male colleagues started sooner'
Lack of role models	'A lack of successful role models who have leveraged their strengths as a female rather than diminished them to get on'

	'Trying to identify women who are an example'
Lack of mentors	'Identifying mentors to support career development'
Work–life balance	'Balancing personal life and career' 'Attempting to be all things to all people i.e. running a home and a career'

Advice to young women

The advice to young women was, predictably, broad and sometimes contradictory. It reflects the relative optimism or pessimism of respondents regarding women's ability to succeed in a corporate environment. Table 4.2 summarises the main themes and quotes.

These open questions revealed new themes. Some are quite striking and some of the recommendations from successful women to emerging leaders may in fact constitute two other possible coping strategies:

- Work ethic: working hard, being patient and taking opportunities.
- Gender behaviour: have a clear strategy when overcoming issues of sexual stereotyping.

However, comments from the participants regarding these two strategies opened up several questions and would benefit from further research. For instance, should women work hard to overcome stereotypes or simply because that is what expected at senior level? Also, the gender behaviour advice was generally supportive ('retain your womanly mannerisms') but sometimes potentially contradictory ('do not go down the womanly wiles route').

Implications when Coaching Women to Lead and organisational support

As all eight coping strategies are statistically significant and remain valid throughout a woman's career, it is worth

Table 4.2 Grouped themes and examples – advice to young women

Theme	Example quotes
Confidence	
Belief in self	'Have confidence and believe in yourself and you'll go so far in your career' 'Stay confident and strong and always believe in yourself'
Awareness of strengths	'Start by evaluating personal strengths' 'Get clarity on strengths and weaknesses'
Perseverance	
Influence of others	'Don't worry about what other people say' 'Don't let anyone tell you that you can't do it!'
Authenticity	'Try not to compromise on what you feel is important'
Stick to goals	'Be clear about the goals you want to achieve in life'
Work ethic	
Patience	'Take time before you react to situations, requests, issues, etc. Pause and listen'
Opportunities	'Be open minded to every opportunity' 'Take risks'
Work	'Work hard, offer to do additional projects, become known for delivering' 'Work harder than you've ever worked in your life, no matter what the task or role'
Education	'Get as many skills as possible' 'Take seminars not just on the subject of business but also on the communication and skills needed to succeed'
Gender behaviour	
Femininity	'Keep your femininity; don't try to be a man'
Equality	'Expect no special treatment' 'Don't use reduced hours/childcare as an excuse for non-delivery' 'Never lock yourself in the toilet and never cry at the office'
Career progression	Plan your career' 'Research jobs and careers'

Behaviours	
Reputation	'Self-promote'
	'Advertise your own success'
Work style	'Behave like a professional'
	'Look people in the eye'
	'Look for the best performer and benchmark yourself against them'
Personal well-being	
Home/family	'Find a supportive partner'
Happiness	'Follow your dreams and be happy'
	'Ask not what the world needs, ask what makes you come alive and do it, because what the world needs is people who have come alive'
Ambitions	'Know what you want'
	'Evaluate your ambitions'
Emotional advice	
Encouragement	'Go for it!'
	'Don't be afraid to have a great aspiration'
Disappointment	'You can't have it all'
	'Working hard/being good is not enough'
Relational support	
Networking	'Build strong, robust networks and maintain a good reputation with the people in the network'
	'Talk to everyone and maintain contacts throughout your career'
Role models	'Identify strong characters with traits you admire'
Mentors	Seek-out mentors and role models – an easy way to pick up lots of useful advice and guidance'
Organisational dynamics	
Culture	'The guys work the system more effectively, know how to get around the rules'
Politics	'Understand the unsaid'
	'Learn the politics'
	'Become a key-player'

exploring further the implications of each of them. Each strategy can be considered in terms of its relevance to coaching (C) or to the employing organisation (O). This is how we could summarise our perspective on each of them:

Family and career balance	C, O
Corporate culture	O
Systematic investment in career and development	C, O
Confidence	C
Knowledge of own strengths	C
Networking	C, O
Role models	O
Career planning	C, O

Let us analyse each in turn.

Family and career balance

There is plenty of evidence that the belief that building a career equals sacrificing a family life holds women back from moving into senior positions. This is a clear area where the full arsenal of coaching, mentoring, networking with role models inside and outside the organisation should be deployed.

When considering young Generation Y managers, their mix of higher confidence, comfort with technology and explicit need for development may make them consider the WLB conundrum in a very different way to that of the previous generation of senior women. They are less likely to accept corporate politics and games. Companies can help through changing WLB policies as well as the development of internal networks.

Because the family–career balance lasts through the majority of a woman's career, it is also appropriate for executive coaching. Specific techniques are developed in Chapter 6.

Corporate culture

A good understanding of corporate culture is essential for women in their career progression. Everyone has a definition of corporate culture, but some simple ones include 'a set of understandings or meanings shared by a group of people', or 'the rules for behaviour in the organisation'. In many organisations, the culture is still based on a set of values and norms around the 'white male heritage'. If women can learn about the social conventions associated with these cultures, they have a much better chance of knowing what to do and when to get on in their careers.

Organisations should take the lead in this area, signposting clearly what constitutes desirable and undesirable behaviour (and preferably tying up behaviours to senior management compensation!). It is worth noting, however, that women *are* also the culture and should take ownership of culture change. This is a complex subject as it is linked with the presence/absence of a critical mass of women at the relevant level of management as discussed in Chapter 2.

A key driver of culture is the informal channels that communicate it. This takes us back to *networking* and how coaching can play a key role (see that section).

Systematic investment in career development

There are many interesting articles on the role and composition of training and developing women: some scholars advocate same-sex training for example to mimic the higher efficacy of same-sex education for girls, while others focus more on the usefulness of indirect learning of norms and culture in mixed groups. There is, however, agreement on the need for women to invest some of their very precious time in training and development (with often the equivalent of two full-time jobs, the opportunity cost of training time may look quite high to many women). Organisations may offer the menu but coaching can certainly be useful in helping decide what is the best investment at various career stages. It is not unusual for example for executives (both men and women) to focus on beefing up their weaknesses by taking training courses in areas that they will never use. A coach can help focus on strengths to boost confidence and focus the development on the likely needs of the executives' career instead.

Confidence

'Internal locus of control' is defined as the belief that one can have a personal influence on events in life. Its opposite state is 'learned helplessness' or the belief that nothing will change no matter what we do. This is largely the bread and butter of the coaching profession, so implications are evident. It is also confirmed in the research literature: Bell and Huffington (2008) for example argue that coaching is critical to obtaining leadership positions. What is particularly remarkable is that this is a theme that affects most women during most of their career (as demonstrated in the quantitative findings). A large section of Chapter 6 is devoted to techniques to increase confidence.

Knowledge of own strengths

Most successful women are well aware of their capabilities. However, in a male-dominated environment in which women continuously have to prove their worth, this knowledge of their strengths can be a useful source of perseverance. The belief in one's capabilities to successfully complete a task has been linked to success at work and is also important for women who want to move up the corporate ladder.

Furthermore, feedback on performance is just as important for achieving promotion because it provides women with a better knowledge of their strengths. Learning what these are, or how other people see them, can help women to use them to their full potential to further their careers.

From a coaching perspective, there are many established tools and approaches, in particular those derived from Positive Psychology. Again, turn to Chapter 6 for examples.

Networking

It is an unwritten rule that relationships are key to performance and success in organisations – and may be even more
important to women than men at work, as well as in life. 'The
process of seeking and providing supportive contacts for
work purposes', or networking, is constantly provided as a
strategy for overcoming women's barriers to senior positions.
One of the major ways in which this works for women is
by reducing the isolation in which they frequently find themselves in a male-dominated environment. Networks also provide a social support system, feedback and the opportunity
to gain influence. Learning to build, maintain and use a network is an important strategy in overcoming barriers to
higher positions.

The organisation can help by building relevant networks
(see Chapter 8), but coaching also has an important role
to play: many women are resistant to networking. A whole
section of Chapter 6 is devoted to building strong networks
and overcoming personal resistance, including psychological
and practical aspects.

Role models

Role models have long been considered important in helping
women progress their careers – seeing a woman on the board
sends out a powerful message to other women that it can be
achieved. Role models fulfil a 'powerful longing for someone
to guide through the contradictions we face' – they also
set an example of how women can deal with the barriers to
higher positions.

As will be shown in Chapter 5, it is not only the scarcity
of role models that is an issue but also what they represent:
many women have reached the top by 'out-manning' the men
and are viewed as scary. More than the quantity of role
models, it is the quality that counts. An extended discussion
on how to seek out relevant role models both inside and
outside the organisation is presented in Chapter 6. This is
obviously also one area where companies can help directly.
Many, for example, are asking all their senior executives to

mentor several young managers each year. Companies also need to manage the pipeline of future role models actively as seen in Chapter 2.

Career planning

For everyone, having a clear sense of direction, of where your career is heading, is beneficial. Studies suggest that it is even more beneficial for women – and that this may be because they tend to do less career planning than men. In general, male managers engage in long-term career planning, while women are more focused on the daily aspects of their jobs. This may put them at a disadvantage as they can all too often remain in jobs with no prospect of promotion because they haven't given much thought to their future. In many multinationals today, career planning for women is taking on a much higher priority as it is a recognised way of helping them progress.

A coach can help too: for example making explicit which aspirations are required and which – if any – Big Scary Job is required to get there is also important. This is a complex area: men often change careers to find meaning after having achieved early success in their competitive career. For many women real meaning comes from outside work: the challenges are different and come at a different time.

Our interviews in the next chapter – the other piece of our research – explain these challenges in greater detail, while the organisational implications are the object of Chapter 8.

In search of role models – conversations with exemplary women

If neither God nor Lord Byron understands the direction of women, then insight can only be gained by asking women themselves.

In the research reported in Chapter 4, women spoke repeatedly of the need for role models, mentors and examples, who could encourage women to pursue their careers. We decided to find some role models of our own. We conducted 25 in-depth, structured interviews with a wide range of women from different organisations, professions and stages of their careers. Their common characteristic is that they have all 'made it' and can potentially be strong role models to emerging female leaders both inside and outside their organisations. We are indebted to them for the time they gave, the thought they put into their responses and the honesty with which they addressed the questions. However, that very honesty created its own problem: because women are so few and far between, especially at the most senior levels, they could be easily identified from their stories. We would have had to edit some of their responses because of the impact their opinions might have if their colleagues read the book. So, we decided to pool some of the information from all our respondents and keep the case studies anonymous. You can read about the fantastic women who took part in Appendix 2. If you are one of them – then yet again – thank you.

Interview process

We did not choose our respondents to mimic the proportions of the business population: we simply used our networks to recommend women in a corporate environment who had a story to tell and could be considered as role models. Also, we avoided choosing clients so as to get a truer perspective on the prevalence of coaching among senior women. We conducted 25 structured interviews. Believe us, all were highly engaging, sometimes fascinating. We have regrouped the 14 selected interviews into five categories in order to facilitate comparisons. These are:

- City women
- HR executives
- Lawyers
- Women working in the not-for-profit sector
- Marketing and PR professionals.

Although each interview turned out to be unique and fascinating in its own way, on each occasion we asked this series of open questions:

- Tell me about yourself.
- What has been important to you as a woman in your career?
- What difference has it made being a woman?
- What has contributed to your success so far?
- What would have been useful in your career?
- What advice would you give young women starting out in their careers?
- What advice would you give women as they reach middle management?
- What are the most important factors when you reach the board?
- What is needed to ensure more women leaders in the future?
- What coaching have you had?
- When would you most have valued coaching?
- What would be the most significant areas for coaching?

The City women

Senior bankers or professionals specialising in financial services and working in the City of London.

1. Alice

Tell me about yourself

Alice has over 20 years of experience in the financial services sector. She started in the banking industry in New York doing 'really cool stuff' and was one of the youngest people picked to work on the integration of banks that had been bought. She spent 10 years in consumer banking. After a break to study for an MBA at IMD and to have her son, she worked freelance but found it quite lonely. She had several job offers and made her choice based on her liking for the managing partner. She works at board and CEO level on core strategic issues in the cards, retail banking and long-term savings sectors.

What has been important to you as a woman in your career?

There are not enough senior women out there, therefore women perceive themselves as quite special. Another woman can be seen as a threat. Until a critical ratio is reached, this will continue to be a problem. Women can be their own worst enemies in the workplace. They make many value judgments. As a result she doesn't automatically trust senior women. Women are all very different – from the girly girls, earth mothers to the ball breakers. Because women are much more heterogeneous it makes it hard to achieve critical mass. Men, being more homogeneous, form a more united front. It is harder for women to find the common ground.

What difference has it made being a woman?

Life was made very difficult for her from the start in her current job. Behaviour was almost on the level of the hazing seen in military schools. She observed that men would not have been treated in the same way. She realises that she threatened them and upset their equilibrium. Her belief is that men do not like smart women and many do not accept strong women. Male colleagues did not know how to relate to a woman who acted like an equal. They were just not used to it. As a result, they would flirt, compliment or try sexual innuendo rather than adopt straightforward professional behaviour. She noticed that some women coped by playing men's games. Used to being the only woman, these women developed 'the only hen in the hen house' attitudes and found it hard to accommodate other women. She found that older European men could cope best when women were subservient, but not if the women proved better than them, i.e. when women 'got above their station'. She was very senior when she joined her current organisation. As a result she had not come up through the hierarchy. She hadn't learned to 'suck up'. She was starting a financial services practice and got the job because no one else wanted it. Although she built the business from zero to millions, she was taken on below partner level and had to jump through hoops for promotion. It was very hard but she made partner within ten months. Although she brought in more money than her male peers, no equivalent man was taken in below partner level. Today only 10–11 per cent of the 200 partners are women. She still has a difficult time. She has a great team but finds the old boys' club is still operating in the firm. There has been no positive advantage to being a woman. In the USA, there are many more senior women so they are less like fish out of water. In the UK, it is different. Young women need role models and support, which is seriously lacking.

What has contributed to your success so far?

- A great husband. She couldn't do it without him covering her hours.
- Very hard work.
- Academic credentials – she has made a big investment in her studies which constituted sweat equity.
- Very clear vision, strategy and practical applications.
- A high focus.

- A desire to keep growing, stretching and changing.
- Doing great work, including building client relationships.

What would have been useful in your career?

- A better understanding of networking. She was never willing to allocate the time to it.
- Better developed political radar – women often have an antipathy to fatuous politics but she should have realised that who you knew was more important than what you knew or how hard you worked.
- Understanding what makes people tick. She didn't feel good at this, had little patience and saw it as a terrible waste of time.

What advice would you give young women starting out in their careers?

- Learn as much as possible. Expose yourself to every opportunity. Take every training course.
- Have as many accomplishments as possible.
- Don't plan your life, i.e. avoid saying, 'I have to do this by this time'.
- Live in the moment. Women get obsessed by what age and stage they are at – let things happen.

What advice would you give women as they reach middle management?

- Don't undersell or underestimate yourself. Work to get alignment.
- Build a very strong network. It is your biggest asset. It is unique and no one can replicate it. Give back to others in order to keep it going.
- Build your brand – what it is and how you grow it.

What are the most important factors when you reach the Board?

- Map every single person you need to influence. Make cogent plans for winning them over.

- Develop a value proposition for yourself – men over-promote, women under-promote.

What is needed to ensure more women leaders in the future?

- Ensure that the pipeline is filled.
- Retain as many women as possible.
- The confidence of the younger women coming up ought to make a difference.
- Women need to support each other through their networks.
- Flexibility is almost impossible in senior consulting – but you have to make it work.
- Men can only do it as they have domestic PAs (aka: wives). Women need to arrange something similar, so they are not attempting to do it all.
- Grassroots change all the way up.

What coaching have you had?

None.

When would you most have valued coaching?

- The period between 29 and 32 when shifting to a more senior role.
- Now – as a partner – when trying to work out how to get to the next level, i.e. how do I manage the next 20 years?

What would be the most significant areas for coaching?

- Confidence.
- How do you manage men's perception of you without feeling compromised or losing your principles.
- A structured, disciplined, academic approach.
- Navigate how to do the right things with rigour but also how to do the window dressing.
- You need to work out how to play the role until you can change the system.

2. Bernice

Tell me about yourself

Born in the south of France, eldest of four children. Parents in education – she should go into medicine or education but not finance. She didn't know whom to ask about joining a bank. Joined Andersen Consulting for three years, discovered the City, investment banking, consulting. She has been a banker ever since, leaving and setting up new teams at regular intervals. Joined CSFB just before the merger with Lehman brothers. Was there eight years – one of the longest serving until the winding up in 2008. She has recently set up with a new team, which launched in May 2009. She started her career by chance as it all sounded interesting and exciting and stayed. She is married with two children.

What has been important to you as a woman in your career?

- Key drivers were to have something interesting, intelligent and rewarding.
- The search for financial independence.

What difference has it made being a woman?

- At first very few women in the City – advantage at beginning. She was the only one so they all know your name. She was noticed and brought on to projects.
- Able to read people's behaviour and use it to advantage.
- Once competing for leadership positions it got tougher – as not in the same network circles, however hard you try.
- Senior man looks at the guys, sees himself and identifies the characteristics he is looking for.
- Took longer to get to senior positions. Lost the advantage for a couple of years or more.
- Now well known and has developed an identity which differentiates and it helps.
- If you are not in the inner circle some business decisions are made without you.
- Generally, OK when things are going well but in the credit crunch people went into survival mode, choosing the

brotherhood in difficult times – revert to those like you, so all male.

What has contributed to your success so far?

- Personal characteristics like hard work ethics (from Dad).
- The ability to make friends (from Mum).
- The determination to never give up.
- Being optimistic by nature.
- A function of the time – only foreigner in the team. Bringing what others didn't have.
- The willingness to move to new places, even when it didn't always make sense.

What would have been useful in your career?

Having a mentor to teach how to navigate the organisation better and avoid the pitfalls.

What advice would you give young women starting out in their careers?

- Do your due diligence beforehand. Speak to people with no axe to grind – ask about life, job, environment – e.g. so you know exactly what you are getting into.
- The job should be very important part of your life but not your whole life – she waited till established in her career to have children but would make a different decision if she had her time again.

What advice would you give women as they reach middle management?

- Adapt and do exciting, well-paid work without sacrifice.
- Make the right choices.
- Want it all but you may have to have it sequentially.

What are the most important factors when you reach the Board?

- When your leadership skills are important you hit a new difficulty. Women do not have the same appetite or

enjoyment of power. They lead as a means to an end (it is not their goal to be boss as an end in itself); men enjoy power and want to exercise it at every opportunity so they practise whenever they can.
• Be more conscious of the experience men gain.

What is needed to ensure more women leaders in the future?

• You get good at something through practice. Girls are encouraged in social skills but boys in aspects of leadership. Teach girls to be leaders from an early age.
• Respect differences – women won't love power – educate both sides as to style. A diverse team will be easier. All men need a male leadership style.
• Change the way organisations work. In big organisations one needs to work long hours. Women will never want to make up 50 per cent of the leaders if this stays the same.
• The crisis in banking ought to be good for women. In the past, short-term performance through high risk taking has been rewarded, this needs to change.

What coaching have you had?

Only internal training.

When would you most have valued coaching?

• At times of change.
• When going on maternity leave.
• When returning from maternity leave – needed to communicate ambition more as was likely to be passed over as boss had made wrong assumptions.
• When facing a difficult situation – became defensive, hurt and stopped communicating – a bad year.

What would be the most significant areas for coaching?

• At an early stage, out of University – understand how to succeed, need for qualities you haven't used before.
• Work out rules of the game – not what you do but so many

other factors – how you present and sell yourself. How to go from meritocracy to learn how you will be judged.
- In the junior/mid years all the leadership issues come into play in order to reduce the revolving door.
- Any period of change – organisational/individual career – how to influence those over whom you have no direct control.

3. Caitlin

Tell me about yourself

Has been with the bank 26 years. She wanted to leave school and earn. At school it was just assumed that all the girls were going to have careers. The bank was like family – very hierarchical. You had to be good at everything so they moved you around. Always focused on career – wanted to conquer the world. She went into specialism in the mid 1990s – lending. At first she hated it and refused to go. She was told she would never have a career if she didn't do it. Went down the ops and lending route. Asked to do one of the first operational management roles. Her career progressed fast with the bank culture as it became less hierarchical. If you were good, you would be put where you could succeed.

What has been important to you as a woman in your career?

- Being valued – above all else.
- Wanting to get out of bed every day to go to work.
- No positive discrimination, so never an advantage or a disadvantage.
- No glass ceiling – that she experienced.
- Could not imagine doing this job with children.
- Couldn't do without her husband – he is her sanity check.

What difference has it made being a woman?

- You pull different levers. Use your femininity to your advantage.

- You are more attuned to the emotional aspects of what is happening around you. Men aren't as conscious or choose not to be.
- You are more sensitive to things that happen and can over-analyse.
- You worry about what you have to do to be successful.
- You strategise more. Want to do every job well.

What has contributed to your success so far?

- Hard work.
- Being very clear about what motivates you and what you enjoy.
- Knowing you are valued.
- Making a difference.
- Working through people.
- Wanting to maintain a certain lifestyle – subconscious vision.
- Other people's belief.
- Not wanting to say 'no' even if you don't believe you can do it.
- Being given a challenge.

What would have been useful in your career?

- Can feel like you are the only person experiencing something. It would have been good to compare notes with other women.
- A female peer group, relationships and a network – where you can be honest and admit when you feel out of your depth.

What advice would you give young women starting out in their careers?

- Don't get hung up on being a woman or glass ceilings.
- Build your brand on what you are good at and be flexible.
- Build a good network – not just women.

*What advice would you give women as they reach
middle management?*

- Find people better than you and get them to work for you.
- Try to be good at everything you do.

*What are the most important factors when you reach
the Board?*

- To help other women.
- Be accessible.
- Don't be scary.
- Be aware of how you impact.

*What is needed to ensure more women leaders in
the future?*

- It is difficult if you want children.
- Good role models.
- The culture is very macho and not 9–5, so hard with a family.
- Flexibility, role modelling won't change while it is male dominated.

What coaching have you had?

- Internal – not very good.
- External for nine months – regarding internal politics, environment, good feedback, insight from different angles.

When would you most have valued coaching?

At the very first stage of managing people, as leadership is hardest.

What would be the most significant areas for coaching?

- How to be a respected leader while being yourself.
- How to keep it real.
- How not to be scary as it is hard to be a role model.
- How to stop being self-effacing.
- How to connect (men don't have to think about this).

4. Daphne

Tell me about yourself

She comes from a high-achieving corporate background: she has reached very senior positions in investment banking, corporate finance and consulting – Morgan Stanley, JP Morgan and McKinsey. She decided that what made companies successful were their diversity practices and culture. She had two children and felt like an almost extinct species trying to combine motherhood and a demanding job. She studied for an MBA as she felt this would broaden her career options – a low percentage of women in finance do MBAs. At first in her career, companies were great at ensuring that there were equal numbers of men and women but this proved a superficial intervention.

What has been important to you as a woman in your career?

- Having role models – especially women as their example is more relevant.
- Coaching through difficult transitions, although women are under-coached.
- Understanding that while assertiveness is respected in a man, it is regarded as less good in a woman.
- Flexibility – working with a firm that allows you to work in different ways.
- A supportive and encouraging partner. Too many professional women have partners who say they don't need to work.
- Confidence.

What difference has it made being a woman?

You are more aware of being different which can be an advantage as you stand out and are more memorable. The disadvantage is that women are often more tentative in their approach – not wanting to rock the boat or being seen as the 'squeaky wheel'. Women also have what is so often described as the 'touchy feely' stuff, i.e. a wider set of leadership styles and tools at their disposal ensuring that they feel authentic. There is always the challenge of the guilt women create for themselves and society dishes out, carrying the huge burden of home, family, team, partner.

In the USA there is terrible maternity leave but they are much better at getting women back into work and keeping them there. Combining work and family is a very important part of her identity but it is very hard and requires a great deal of compromise. When her oldest child was discovered to have very special needs she realised she could not be the next head of McKinsey and had to reassess her assumptions. Until that point she felt she had had a charmed career.

What has contributed to your success so far?

- Resilience – learning from mistakes and not dwelling on them. Persevering. Women tend not to do this well as they take things more personally – stuff happens!
- Hard work; elbow grease until she became good at something.
- Good education. Graduating with honours led to confidence and to jobs.
- Leadership style – a good team player and builder which had a big impact, gaining people's confidence and getting results quickly.
- Good communication skills – convincing people and selling self.

What would have been useful in your career?

- More access to coaching – always had to ask.
- More of a leadership curriculum than there was in the past.
- Mentoring – always had to seek out mentors and convince them to do it – it took time to figure out.
- Companies struggle not to be heavy handed but more guidance would help.

What advice would you give young women starting out in their careers?

- Have more confidence. Don't hold yourself back.
- No one will manage your career for you. Do it yourself.

- Don't lose your femininity – there are advantages to standing out and wearing pink!

What advice would you give women as they reach middle management?

- You can have it all but you just can't do it all at the same time.
- Key years are the 30s and early 40s – women need to proactively manage their profile and build their network. Being good at the job just isn't enough.
- Be aware of your choices. Not marrying or having children are choices. Don't be passive.
- Be aware of the mummy track.

What are the most important factors when you reach the Board?

- Realise that you are an important role model. Hundreds and thousands of women will be watching you.
- Give back – reach down, help others. If you behave like a Queen Bee it will give you a very bad reputation.

What is needed to ensure more women leaders in the future?

- All too often, senior people hire in their own image. There is a vast pool of highly qualified, committed women who won't have the same linear career path as the men and as a result will bring something different to the role.
- Open-mindedness about what a woman brings to the table, e.g. they may have had career breaks but have the same degree of experience, maturity and are ready to prove themselves.
- More Board nominations and promotions. Women do not always sell themselves as well as men and can be more modest about their talent and their goals. Companies need to take a more holistic view.
- Awareness of opportunities. HR needs to be transmitting the right information especially at the more junior levels.
- Stretch assignments. Women are less likely to get them

and they are vital to their career. Assumptions are made and not checked.

- The media could be more helpful and constructive. There are many good news stories about female role models but they don't tend to be what sells.
- Better role models who demonstrate a variety of paths to success.
- Flexibility can be double edged. While many women could benefit, it puts the onus on women rather than changing working practices more radically. There can be an impact on women's opportunities and sense of identity.
- Legislation can backfire and make women less attractive to hire, e.g. maternity leave.

What coaching have you had?

- Early on as a new manager/consultant at McKinsey – it was offered to all managers around 28 years of age. It dealt with the importance of handling people well, so emphasised soft skills: selling yourself. Using 360 feedback and questionnaires, it helped her to develop insight into her traits, was informative and empowered her.
- She was hitting her head against the promotion ceiling, despite meeting all the criteria. She found it difficult to get candid feedback about what she might be doing wrong. Coaching gave the chance to think through other people's agenda and to contemplate how to raise her profile. She realised the promotion had little to do with her achievements and much more to do with how she sold herself.
- Five years later, when establishing her new business, she needed a sounding board. Coaching proved very different from the previous times and she achieved much greater self-awareness.

When would you most have valued coaching?

- When returning from maternity leave. Her confidence was very vulnerable and she had concerns about the clashing identities of mother and working woman.
- When she felt she had stumbled and was not achiev-

ing promotion on a fast track, which knocked her back. Coaching would have got her through this stage much faster.

- In a new chief operating officer position, technical coaching would have been valuable. She had strategic experience but not grassroots knowledge. Coaching would have got her up to speed fast and established her credibility and strengthened her confidence.

What would be the most significant areas for coaching?

- Confidence – even the most eminent women have lower confidence than their male peers. It seems to be fundamental to the DNA of being a woman.
- Helping women understand that their careers are likely to be non-linear or more of a labyrinth – and as a result more challenging. If it were a jigsaw men would have 50 pieces. Women have 100. It is still the same jigsaw, women just need to be more persistent and work harder at putting the pieces into place.
- Developing different styles. Realising that they are more likely to stand out, women need to think through what feels natural and develop some of the styles that may not.

Coaching implications

This successful and formidable group of City women were unequivocal in their recognition of the challenges facing women, especially when they combined motherhood and City careers. In their personal lives, they saw a need to choose very carefully a partner who would encourage and support their careers and to make conscious decisions about whether, when and how to have children rather than fitting it around their work. It was delightful that some of these potentially daunting women were very wary of 'those scary women' and cautioned women to support and encourage others whenever they could. In terms of coaching, the following came out strongly:

- Women should have coaching at all levels.
- There is a particular need for coaching both pre- and

post-maternity leave in order to plan well and make a rapid and effective re-entry.

• Confidence is a fundamental coaching need for women however well they are doing.

HR executives

5. Evelyn

Tell me about yourself

Evelyn's career started in the hotel business, then she worked for corporate information specialists in the UK and in New York. After that she moved to a global business that was developing luxury brands and had enough courage to put an HR director on its board.

What has been important to you as a woman in your career?

'You can't take anything for granted.' She has had great mentors and the best bosses who have encouraged her. Even the worst bosses had confidence in her but she had to overcome classic female self-doubt. Mentors had to be male as there were so few women around. It has been critical to build trust and influence in order to become credible – taking ownership, accountability and delivering. She feels that 'as soon as you think "I need to be like them to survive", i.e. men, then you lose your authenticity'. The compromise will show.

What difference has it made being a woman?

• You have a different perspective generally – a more rounded thinker.
• You take a holistic view of things which is a very valuable contribution to the picture – not softer or nicer.
• Are more likely to be looking ahead for contingencies and the next thing.
• Can show perceived weaknesses more, unlike the men you work with.
• Use network – family, friends – to talk through, weep without someone trying to solve/fix.

- Are less competitive in some ways. Happy to ask for help without loss of face. More comradely.

What has contributed to your success so far?

- Having the opportunities.
- Taking the opportunities.
- A curiosity and willingness to learn.
- Straight talking helps in a man's world. (Can be too direct with women.)
- Mentoring.
- Coaching – formal and informal.
- Learning from mistakes.
- A flexible influencing style – understand individuals and adapt.
- Being intuitive.

What would have been useful in your career?

- Role models in a variety of aspects of life.
- Being more flexible in career rather than choosing one path to follow. Women need to commit to the path for the moment, and not be too rigidly fixed.

What advice would you give young women starting out in their careers?

- Do something that inspires you and that you enjoy doing, not what someone else wants you to do.
- Take risks and go for it.

What advice would you give women as they reach middle management?

- The next step up can seem big. Don't wait until you are ready. You can't practise it one level down. No one is ready.
- Remember who you are and what has made you successful to this point. Don't change that. Retain authenticity and develop responsibility.
- You are on a steep learning curve and you need to deliver.
- Have trust in the system. If it flagged you up then trust it and grow faith in yourself.

What are the most important factors when you reach the Board?

- You have the responsibility to be a role model to all people in the organisation. Show them what a successful woman looks like.
- Accept that women are different – leverage the strength that that gives.
- Find a good coach – especially if you are the only woman on the board.

What is needed to ensure more women leaders in the future?

- More flexibility in the working environment. There are now more senior women having children than before.
- Mechanics – the system is changing. How can you do really good interim cover? Very senior women need excellent cover.
- Focus on leveraging people's strengths. Give them visibility. Highlight their strengths (sometimes seen as 'soft') and the value they add.
- Some industries don't automatically attract women. Find ways of having more women in the emerging leaders pool.
- Accelerate the growth of women and convert them into senior positions sooner.

What coaching have you had?

- When stepping up to a more senior position learning to shift up a gear.
- On moving to the USA with particular focus on managing the cultural differences where there were very traditional men.
- Becoming a chairperson, embarking on fundraising and networking.

When would you most have valued coaching?

- Earlier on when making career choices that would determine much of her working life.
- Earlier at each stage with different purpose at each time.

What would be the most significant areas for coaching?

- Confidence – self-belief and a balanced view of self.
- Assertiveness as opposed to aggressiveness – how to get the balance right.
- How to leverage strengths.
- How to allow yourself some weaknesses. You don't need to be the whole package.
- In developing your image. How do you turn yourself out while keeping your femininity – as it is a strength?
- Physical presentation. How you come across, manage conversations, interrupting, choosing the right seat at the table – all of which can be power plays.

6. Frances

Tell me about yourself

She is a typical woman, over-delivering because she is packing as much as possible into the hours at her disposal because she earns more, she is the breadwinner of the family. Home life is demanding. She has found her passion in her work and never stops thinking about it. Her career was not planned. She just tends to throw herself in and aims to get the best out of everything. As a result she feels really lucky about where her career has taken her.

What has been important to you as a woman in your career?

Latterly the most important thing has been networks and friendships. She has so many contacts that she could fill the Albert Hall! Before she had some internal networks but these were not really strategic. Mentors have looked out for her, ensuring that there were people there at strategic times who could influence on her behalf.

What difference has it made being a woman?

- You are pretty obvious. As you become more senior you stand out more, e.g. in investment banking she was the only woman.

- It is so important not to stand out for the wrong reasons. 'Don't wear such a strong perfume or lipstick, wear a short skirt or such a low neckline that that is all you can be remembered for.'
- She was valued for her contribution because she was a woman and had a different approach to problem solving compared with the traders and salesmen.
- Being different added value, even if not everyone perceived it.
- People treated her better. They didn't expect so much of a woman and so any achievement was noticed in the early days.

What has contributed to your success so far?

- Incredible resilience.
- Naivety – which can be a strength or a weakness. She just took things at their face value with no thought to underlying meanings.
- A sense of humour.
- The ability to balance work with the enormous demands outside work.
- Exposure to a very wide range of people.
- The capacity to bounce back from diversity.

What would have been useful in your career?

- Better political savvy – being aware of other people's lives.
- Caution.
- Less wearing of her heart on her sleeve.
- Being aware of how she comes across.
- Being a man! – e.g. having an interest in sport which would have made it easier to establish rapport and relationships.

What advice would you give young women starting out in their careers?

- Network – internal and external. Think broadly and use every opportunity. Follow up every contact. It is worth as much as investing in a really good bra!

- Have a plan and a vision as it gives you a better feel for where you want to go.
- Watch, listen, learn and ask people questions about what they do.
- Learn the unwritten rules – no one will hand you a manual. This is where a mentor comes in handy.

What advice would you give women as they reach middle management?

- Have the difficult conversations. Articulate your views. Make sure you have airtime.
- Take ownership even if it is unfair but avoid being a victim.
- Have clear aspirations and devise possible routes to success. Look for opportunities to have necessary conversations where you can state your ambitions.

What are the most important factors when you reach the Board?

- Prepare yourself. You need a demanding skills set. Find out in advance.
- Find a non-exec as mentor.
- Be strategic.

What is needed to ensure more women leaders in the future?

- Men have to have the babies!
- Women need a licence to make choices.
- A tipping point when there are enough women to make a difference.
- Portfolio careers.
- The sharing of home life and family responsibilities.

What coaching have you had?

- Informal coaching internally and externally as a third party who can view any situation from a different dimension.

When would you most have valued coaching?

- When taking on more stretch assignments.
- When dealing with conflict and change management.

What would be the most significant areas for coaching?

- Managing conflict while staying authentic.
- Moving from operational to leadership roles and behaviours. Many women hang on to the part of the job they are good at – tried and tested. They need to delegate and move on to the more ambiguous, less transactional side of leadership.

Coaching implications

This powerful group of women emphasised the need to take advantage of being in the minority but cautioned against standing out for the wrong reasons while celebrating the special talents that tend to come with being a woman and encouraged retaining some femininity. There was a strong emphasis on building strategic networks and relationships with both male and female mentors. In terms of coaching needs:

- Women need coaching at every stage of their career in order to make faster transitions.
- They need to learn how to play the game – at least until they have enough power to change the rules.
- Learning how to be authentic.
- Taking risks and moving into leadership behaviour.

The lawyers

7. Gill

Tell me about yourself

Gill pursued law, after toying with a completely different career in the arts. Thirteen years later she became the first partner ever to be made up on a three-day working week in that firm. She has been working flexibly for the last ten years and was made an equity partner in 2004. All of which is still quite rare in the legal profession. She heads up a practice and is relaxed about how or where she works. She has three girls at school, a terrific nanny and now works a four-day week and enjoys one day to herself.

What has been important to you as a woman in your career?

Women have to balance all the time. If part-time working or flexibility had not been available she would have left. Emotional stability is essential in order for her to be enabled to do other things. She still takes one day a week off now more for herself – she plays tennis, etc., which gives her perspective and objectivity. People have faith and confidence in her, so she is able to be herself and is accepted for that rather than fitting into a cookie cutter mentality. Lots of law firms would not have given the support and platform she has had.

What difference has it made being a woman?

- Some women come at things from a very different angle. They don't have the baggage of having to 'climb the career ladder no matter what', so they can question and challenge policies when men might just assume them to be right.
- Women are more creative, people-driven and look at the long-term consequences, whereas men can be more black and white and driven by pure financials.
- Lawyers often share a very specific profile. They tend not to be very intuitive or long-sighted. Men are often very uncomfortable with her challenges. They are not used to it. Women tend to bring up the elephant in the room. They sense what is not being said.
- Women have better developed Emotional Intelligence and so notice body language, subtexts and so are very useful when things get tough in negotiations.
- Men can be very resentful of women. They assume you are just being difficult so you are constantly trying to tread a fine line between playing the rules of the games and being

true to yourself. There are interesting neuro-economic theories. Men have an immediate high performance as testosterone surges but an inability to see longer term consequences at the same time. Women balance this.

What has contributed to your success so far?

- Being good at what I do.
- Having good client skills.
- Having an understanding of the market.
- Being very driven – want to do it well or not at all, so put a lot of energy into the task.
- Really liking people – team partners, clients.
- Being very curious – has a broad appetite for knowing about lots of things – business, HR – all fascinating.
- Having other important things in life so never consumed by work alone.
- Can walk away. Has a 'my day' every week.

What would have been useful in your career?

- To have been a better technical lawyer when younger – learned young who you can bring with you, built strategic relationships but has some anxiety about having skipped technical building blocks as a result.
- Having the respect of peer group.
- Understanding that she is a better lawyer than she believes.

What advice would you give young women starting out in their careers?

- Don't put children on hold while progressing your career – it makes the stakes too high. You will be too disappointed if you don't achieve. Do it when you want to rather than when you think your employers would like it.
- Succeed whether or not you have children.
- It is really, really hard. You are going to need backbone.
- Self-belief is essential. It is a huge investment. You will not always feel like it is worth it.

What advice would you give women as they reach middle management?

- Promotion will not always follow.
- You need very different skills for senior management.
- Keep your perspective because it will impact on your judgment and integrity.
- When studying she had the assumption that you could do anything you wanted. Having children is a real stumbling block to that as you can't keep all the balls in the air.

What are the most important factors when you reach the Board?

- Others aren't going to keep the balls in their air for you – set parameters and commitments you can make.
- You need to be robust and thick skinned.
- Provide a role model that demonstrates skills that a woman can empathise with – most senior women terrify her and are not models to emulate.

What is needed to ensure more women leaders in the future?

- Businesses need to capture women's skills in senior management roles without requiring them to subsume themselves to their career.
- Women still lack confidence to sit at board level and play their part in that space.
- Numbers – they are beginning to change in the right direction.
- Boards need to be more collegiate.
- Women need to be good at working out where the boundaries are as this leads to making compromises which many decide are not worth it if everything else falls out of place.

What coaching have you had?

- Had a male coach who came highly recommended but during five sessions she found he wasn't dealing with the issues she wanted. He focused on five-year plans and clear steps, which were not the main issues for her at that time. He didn't really relate to the issues a woman faces – such as being the only woman on an all male strategic board. Her anxiety and lack of confidence in that context were not dealt with.

When would you most have valued coaching?

- At the times when changing roles.
- When coming back to work after children and working flexibly.
- On management roles.
- When deciding what is next.

What would be the most significant areas for coaching?

- To eliminate self-imposed barriers.
- To build resilience.
- To normalise your position at the senior level.

8. Helen

Tell me about yourself

A litigation lawyer and board member of a law firm, she champions the advancement of women, having recognised the waste caused by losing women when they make up 64 per cent at entry level but have dwindled to only 22 per cent at partner and 14 per cent at equity level. She realised there needed to be a sound business case in order to encourage the structure to move in a direction that would lead to retaining women.

What has been important to you as a woman in your career?

- Having a mentor (male) who gave the support she needed to get up to partner level.
- Having flexibility, as working full-on.
- Liking what you do – a lot.
- Working and having economic independence is very important for women.

What difference has it made being a woman?

- There have been both advantages and disadvantages.
- Opportunities have come because of gender.
- Some clients prefer a man but more lately they prefer women.
- More women have gone into the corporate world as in house lawyers and are instructing more women lawyers.
- Network building – the permeation of women leads to very different conversations at lunch!
- You can be better known in your field

What has contributed to your success so far?

- Just like the turtles on the beach – keeping going!
- Doing it well.
- Ambition. Knowing what you want next and just doing it.
- Recognition of what it takes for someone to be successful. Putting yourself forward and making sure you are in the right place.

What would have been useful in your career?

- Successful senior women as role models. Those who had already got there were less amenable and had partially closed the trap door.

What advice would you give young women starting out in their careers?

- Get as much experience as you can.
- Don't let people let you off.
- Avoid being pigeon-holed or brushed off.

What advice would you give women as they reach middle management?

- Decide what you want. If you want to climb, look around at what people do to get ahead.
- Don't allow people to assume you want to be where you are.
- Be louder about your own successes – no one else will be.

What are the most important factors when you reach the Board?

- Know where you want to go and what you want to achieve.
- Take the path you want.
- Things don't just happen, e.g. non-executive directorships. How do you get them?
- Dress for the next level at every step. Men have a uniform, which leads to assumptions about value. Women are more judged and pigeon-holed so project gravitas in your appearance.

What is needed to ensure more women leaders in the future?

- Micro steps until women leaders are taken as the norm.
- Stopping the moral condemnation about women – especially working mothers.
- Changing the very masculine way of doing work – e.g. decisions made in the pub at the very time when women are needing to make connections.
- Finding ways of networking.
- Getting sufficient numbers through so that women are not seen as exceptional. Forty per cent of her Board is now female.
- Serve the client well by giving them diversity.
- Awareness – if two equal candidates apply for a job then employ the under-represented.
- Every woman bringing someone on.

What coaching have you had?

- Some regarding being the only woman on the Board and to help with the diversity programme.
- How best to lead.

When would you most have valued coaching?

- When changing to the next level on how best to project herself.

What would be the most significant areas for coaching?

- Projecting yourself, avoiding being coy. We instil values of working hard in girls – be good and to wait for opportunities to shine, while boys just tell you how good they are.
- On having confidence in your abilities.
- In managing emotions – women constantly feel guilty about letting their children down. They pay a high emotional price for their careers compared with men.

9. Isabel

Tell me about yourself

Recently retired from her role as the UK managing partner of an international law firm, she started life in suburban America, attending local school and studying economics at a smart university. She didn't know what she wanted to do, married, finished grad school and started her professional career at the eighth largest law firm. It was very progressive – they employed women, democrats, blacks and Jews in the mid 1970s because they believed different people had different contributions to make. Had two children and moved to the UK. Looking back she suspects she might not make the same decisions the second time around and wonders why she made the decisions then, e.g. returning full-time in an extreme job with little children.

What has been important to you as a woman in your career?

The demands were ridiculous, e.g. extremely short maternity leave, but she was determined to succeed. She wanted to be respected as a professional so all the decisions fell out of that. Supportive friends along the way have been critically important. One man believed in her and asked her to head up an important account only 4–5 years out of law school – as company secretary of a board of trustees.

What difference has it made being a woman?

- People were very significant to the amount of pleasure she experienced and her ability to progress.
- She had a real novelty factor as there were so few women. People got a kick out of trying her out and watching her do well.
- She wasn't allowed to do litigation as it 'wasn't a job for a woman' – despite her growing up watching Perry Mason. She wasn't allowed to cross a picket line.
- It was a competitive advantage at first.
- Later as it became more important to play with and think like the boys, it was more difficult as there was no locker room equivalent for her. Fell out of the situations where the opportunities were being created. It became less pleasurable as a result.

What has contributed to your success so far?

- Determination.
- Meeting important people along the way.
- Having pleasure in doing what she was doing. Hard to get up and work hard if not easy to keep enthusiastic.
- Changing the world – a sense of being a pioneer. Heady stuff.
- Law was well regarded back then – felt the role was there to help people in a significant way.

What would have been useful in your career?

- An older female mentor who really understood how the business world worked.
- A good psychologist/therapist – ideal to have that in the business world.

What advice would you give young women starting out in their careers?

- Be clear about whether you like what you are doing – figure out early what you are and what you like.
- Be meaningful.
- Understand the politics of the organisation you are in.

*What advice would you give women once they reach
middle management?*

- If women think they will be rewarded for toiling, they are living a fantasy. It doesn't work that way.
- Review whether you are eager to star.
- Make mid-course corrections if unhappy.
- Get from the job what you need to develop as a person/ woman.
- Fairy tales are insidious teaching women the wrong lessons – Sleeping Beauty and Cinderella are heartbreaks waiting to happen.

*What advice would you give women once they reach
the Board?*

- Just as you become a successful professional woman, you need to re-calibrate.

*What is needed to ensure more women leaders in
the future?*

- The momentum has taken hold so the passage of time will achieve some of it, e.g. US politics – women are making their way to the top echelons in significant numbers.
- A person-by-person approach to talent management so women don't get lost due to overwhelming demands
- Women's initiatives – can't afford for women to do well only to leave when they have children. It's a waste of investment. Need women's initiatives – flexitime and part-time working are only a small part of what needs to be done.
- People need to be able to pursue different trajectories rather than fail at the one traditional version of a career.
- Talent development project focused on them over the broad waterfront of entire career. It is not just associated with having preschoolers. Children need all sorts of things at different stages. Women have to devote a substantial percentage of their time over at least 18 years.

What coaching have you had?

- Episodic re specific issues – varied in quality as not always able to identify the right resources.
- Not all coaches understand the economic, political and personal challenges of being a woman.

When would you have most valued coaching?

- At university – had no understanding of business school or MBAs.
- When she decided to direct her career into an area where the firm had no presence. Had no accurate picture of the magnitude of the task.
- When she moved to London – a very different environment, small office, no profile, hadn't been leading a law firm for 100 years! Very different culture. Help through the transition would have been valuable.

What would be the most significant areas for coaching?

- Institutional – how to be successful. What those jobs entail and what you need to do along the way to be promoted.
- A coach could assist in career planning – over 40-year career, responsible for planning and executing own career. Whether to move, change, have additional education.

Coaching implications

This range of experiences illustrates some of the changes that are happening in the legal profession. Once a profession where part-time work in large law firms was considered unthinkable and hence women left in droves, the more forward thinking are being creative in the way they define working patterns. Women need to consider carefully the attitudes and flexibility of the organisations they are choosing. Specific coaching needs are:

- Ensuring that coaches understand the specific pressures on women and do not automatically assume and attempt to instil male patterns of behaviour.

- Working with women to make sure they develop a sense of presence and are noticed.
- Helping to deal with the emotional impact of balancing home and family.

Not-for-profit sector

10. Jess

Tell me about yourself

Jess heads up an organisation which works with families, employers, children, working parents and carers to find a better balance between responsibilities at home and work, through pragmatic advice giving, research and influencing of policy makers. She joined this organisation once she had a child. The organisation she had previously been working for would make no concessions. It was frowned upon to leave at 5 p.m. This was a very young organisation and at first she was the only person with a child. She has always been in voluntary, campaigning, contributing, making a difference area.

What has been important to you as a woman in your career?

- Getting into a female-led organisation.
- Being a parent gave a fresh way of looking at things. Can't do stupid hours.
- This organisation was the whole point of the women's movement. Dominated by female trustees, and Diversity women. Hasn't had to deal with traditional male aggressive management style.

What difference has it made being a woman?

- Been a natural fit in this role for the last 15 years. Women's contribution is taken for granted in the organisation. Everyone would put equal value on a man or woman but in fact it would possibly be harder for a man.
- The difficulty with domestic partner who referred to her 'wee job'. Taking it more seriously now. However, on the

other hand, the fact that he has a better income has meant
that her low income doesn't matter as much.
- As a woman, easy to stay here as no one else wants her job!
People are attracted by the flexibility. Likes doing things
her own way – as the boss. Someone else might be more
ambitious.
- Overly nice to people.
- Sucked into detail.
- Can get too close and 'mummy' them.

What has contributed to your success so far?

- Luck – being at the right place, right time.
- Having brilliant people in team with very different skills
and talents.
- Can do the motivating stuff, create stability so people stick
around.
- Being friendly, warm and enthusiastic.
- Being clever – intellectual.
- Enjoys coming up with new ideas then delegating.

What would have been useful in your career?

- If she had started in a larger organisation, she could have
learned how to be managed. Would then have helped her
learn how to manage better.
- Had no role models except for some very frightening
women she could not identify with.

What advice would you give young women starting out in their careers?

- Find an organisation that accommodates life outside
of work.
- Choose an organisation where the values fit your own.
- See whether people 'look' like you further up the organisation.

What advice would you give women as they reach middle management?

- Don't reject the organisation if not many women at senior levels.
- Ask yourself do others seem happy or do they worry about family commitments?

What is needed to ensure more women leaders in the future?

- Flexible working.
- Need to have a different pattern and reintegrate family into communities. It isn't just all about having confidence. Needs societal change too. We have raised a generation who are blind to the fact that we have a male model of employment, leading to women walking away and talent being lost.
- Organisations need to value what women bring to them.
- Managers who understand the concept of working families.
- Coaching and mentoring – women downplay their abilities. Need someone to encourage and challenge.
- Conversations need to be had at home.
- People at the top with strategic roles must understand gender diversity, leading to better solutions for the differences between men and women.
- Male role models – doing it differently – many men entering a second marriage choose to do things differently. In the younger generation, men are more open about being fathers.

What coaching have you had?

- Several bouts – not all useful.
- Jungian therapist – re how relationships worked in the team, to reassure her she wasn't completely losing it. Very objective.
- Others tended to impose their solutions. She didn't always recognise that till months later.
- A mentor – to work on a specific issue.

When would you most have valued coaching?

- All the way through. Wouldn't be where she is today if she had had coaching from the start! She would probably be somewhere quite different.
- Took until 7–8 years ago to be very good at anything. It would have accelerated that.
- First half of career always too close to the detail – needed to be challenged to stand back to become a leader.
- Would have left other jobs sooner . . . and perhaps ended up in the theatre!
- Two years into the workplace when women think 'Oh, ****!' as they see men getting on better than them.

What would be the most significant areas for coaching?

- Self-belief – in environments that pretend to be gender neutral but are based on a male model.
- Hard for women to challenge – not seen as pulling their weight or being team players.
- Women are constantly questioning and as a result then pack it in or the organisation doesn't get the best out of them although they are rarely knowingly discriminatory.
- Women need to recognise they are partly responsible by pretending to be blokes on the same terms as the men. Need to make a stand.
- Coaching should be equal for both men and women as they have the same life issues to face. Men should be asked the same questions about life and family as it is assumed women will want to discuss.

11. Kay

Tell me about yourself

Now a member of the House of Lords, holding a senior position in UK politics with a particular interest in women, Kay was the only child of very involved parents and had an inspiring head teacher. She won her first election at school and then had an injury that affected her final years at school. At first she contemplated secretarial college but was useless so entered a merchant bank! She left when she had children. She was always interested in politics and involved locally. She hasn't sought anything out in her career, it has just happened.

What has been important to you as a woman in your career?

- Other women in politics have been very enabling as they understood the struggles – selection, rejection, balancing the job, family and politics.
- Women had their own support system.
- Enlightened men are critical to women's success.
- A supportive and accepting family.

What difference has it made being a woman?

- Not so many around so had high visibility that men didn't have.
- There are a lot of knocks in politics that men take personally but women deal better with (e.g. they can't understand why they weren't chosen).
- Easier to be accepted in the community.
- Intuition has helped.
- Can ask the stupid questions and get away with it.
- Can multitask and multichannel.
- Have finer honed antennae – women pick up the smaller voices.
- Has curiosity/nosiness/interest in people.

What has contributed to your success so far?

- The support of the family.
- The ability to see friends through bad times.
- Able to maintain relationships.
- Enjoying people.
- Working hard and enjoying it.
- A passion for politics – children, schools, women.

What would have been useful in your career?

- A bigger brain.
- More money – worrying about the drain on the household.

- Should have had a remunerative business career first and then gone into politics.

What advice would you give young women starting out in their careers?

- Have some fun in the job – women can be so serious.
- The world won't fall apart if you don't do everything.
- Be a first-class woman not a second-rate man.
- Support one another.
- You have fabulous strengths – believe it.
- Do as much training as you can even if you know it. You will always pick up one useful thing.

What advice would you give women as they reach middle management?

- Never stop learning.
- Read widely not just for training.
- Take real time for yourself.
- Never be afraid to admit you don't know – men don't know either.
- Spot the men that will help (not stab you in the back).
- Never think you are too good to do any small job, e.g. tea, minutes.

What are the most important factors when you reach the Board?

- Be yourself – be congruent.
- Don't hog, be enablers for other women.
- Don't be frightened to ask the obvious questions.
- Men mask insecurities better.

What is needed to ensure more women leaders in the future?

- Programmes for women leaders.
- Legislation/organisation should look at the workforce as a whole. Short-sighted to invest in encouraging women through mentoring and training just to let them drift off.

- Enlightened men realise women make a difference and will do anything they can to help.
- Those who have struggled need to bite their tongues and enable others.
- Need feminine role models.

What coaching have you had?

- Constant development – reading and self-help.

When would you most have valued coaching?

- When she had no money to spend on it – needed pro bono.

What would be the most significant areas for coaching?

- Assertiveness – saying no when you can't do it all, without apologising and agonising.
- Leadership at all levels.
- Public speaking and then how to use it.
- Media skills – so they can become spokeswomen. How you come across is so important.

12. Linda

Tell me about yourself

She works as an agent for social change, making sense of the anti-discrimination laws and helping the business community understand talent. After a primary campaigning role in a charity for six years she became the CEO of a not-for-profit organisation. She believes the personal is political and is about who we are. She brings her own experience to the role having experienced ill-health, surgery and lasting physical disablement. She knows that the biggest barriers are always attitudinal. She is now well known in Whitehall for her work on disability legislation.

What has been important to you as a woman in your career?

Having a sense of balance has been critical. She knows she made some wrong assumptions – such as not having children, which has since become a source of regret but has focused her on how to give and receive love without children. It is important to her that being a woman in business has not detracted from her capacity to have a social life and family connections.

What difference has it made being a woman?

- Seen as softer – but not in a 'wussy' sense. She has gifts and skills that lead to the building of strong relationships.
- It makes it easier to get people to change.
- Within politics, relationships are very important. She understands the principles, ethics and the need to encourage people to do things differently. Men find this harder. Women can be conciliatory and find the third way in negotiations.

What has contributed to your success so far?

- Articulation – developing a narrative through stories and statistics.
- Bloody mindedness.
- Determination.
- Time consciousness.
- It can be extremely hard, harder than for men. Women can't afford to be mediocre.
- Carrying the anger, frustration and hurt regarding injustice drives motivation.

What would have been useful in your career?

- The opportunity to talk about issues while searching for a career path. She won a scholarship for leadership training which gave access to a coach mentor and a learning set but only lasted for one year.
- More opportunities to discuss.

What advice would you give young women starting out in their careers?

- Changes to the economy means you don't need to do 'one size fits all'. Many women of previous generations believed they could not have both a career and children. Those times are past.

- See your career as a series of iterations.
- Capitalise on more fluid structures.
- Be who you are. Stay a woman, rather than becoming a clone. Wear the pink shoes!

What advice would you give women as they reach middle management?

- Focus on your strengths.

What are the most important factors when you reach the Board?

- Develop both content and process.
- Concentrate on what you are good at in relationships.
- Don't be shy. Don't wait too long before contributing. It doesn't have to be perfect.
- Accept you are bound to be in the minority, surrounded by men who like the sound of their own voices.
- Men feel like a divine act put them on the board. Women need to develop their own commanding presence.
- Work to get more women on to boards.
- Don't worry.

What is needed to ensure more women leaders in the future?

- Proportionality in governments. The right percentage of women in senior political positions would help as they would be more mindful of women.
- Opportunity for girls to have a dialogue at school and at university with an emphasis on feminism in education.
- Continual noticing, watching brief on the issue but not more legislation.
- Greater support through professional learning bodies, coaching and mentoring.
- Women must not lose their distinctiveness, vibrancy and edge. They must not water down their strengths.
- Simplify legislation and help employers not to lose integrity and quality.

What coaching have you had?

- Coverdale leadership programme. Had a mentor/coach once a month – felt like Christmas. Had a huge day job and was given this rich goody bag.
- Informal coaching with women who mattered, female business contacts and MPs.

When would you most have valued coaching?

- Right now in growing her own business.
- With an ongoing dilemma – finding constructive thinking time. She is irritating herself and wants to know why she is prevaricating and not making a judgment. A coach will cut right through this.
- Structural opportunity.
- Relationship issues – stakeholders, staffing and handling people correctly.

What would be the most significant areas for coaching?

- Being sure of yourself. Having a solid sense and assumption about your right to be here. Women can be too analytic and introspective and so doubt themselves.
- Caring too much about what people think. Women tend to want things to be consensual. Think 'good enough' rather than absolutism.
- Making tough decisions – again you can't bring everyone with you.
- Developing grit – having the chance to take a mirror to yourself when making assumptions.
- Systematic multitasking – develop thinking agility and also focus for behaviour with a deliberate methodology for what will get done a route map for where you want to go.

13. Mary

Tell me about yourself

Mary is the National Director of a national business-led network of private and public sector organisations working together to promote racial equality within their business.

She started her career in the civil service and worked her way up despite having little ambition or self-belief. Thought she would make it to supervisor level at best. As a young BME (British Minority Ethnic) woman she had to work even harder to convince people but one man especially encouraged her. Her performance got her noticed, once technical competence got her in. She realised the need to be on show and find opportunities. People saw her potential. She made a point of being around where people were and getting into conversation knowing they would remember her. She had four years in a very public role and as the only BME she really got noticed. Eighty per cent of the people she was dealing with were men. She was therefore quite novel. She knew she wanted to work on equality, to campaign and to talk to people on the ground. She now has all this.

What has been important to you as a woman in your career?

- Had to succeed. If she failed she knew she would be slamming the door on others.
- Relationship skills – connecting to others, gaining trust especially of senior men who felt there was no one they could trust and who later gave her support and protection.
- Being discreet.
- Being a perfectionist.
- Genuinely caring about the organisation.

What difference has it made being a woman?

- Has made things more difficult – although she has met some great women along the way.
- Being heard.
- Having ideas 'stolen' by men – had to learn not to care as long as it got done.
- Breaking new ground.
- Getting used to being in the minority.
- Being able to go under the radar.

What has contributed to your success so far?

- Great people along the way – unofficial mentors, coaches, leaders who spotted talent, who knew the culture and guided her.
- Actively pursuing learning.
- Having champions and advocacy.
- Giving feedback to senior people who wouldn't normally get any.
- Investing in relationships.
- Being prepared to step out of her comfort zone when she didn't want to.
- Disappointments that lead to learning and radical change.
- Drive to learn, be better.
- Being totally immersed in the job.

What would have been useful in your career?

- At start didn't know any of this – it all occurred accidentally.

What advice would you give young women starting out in their careers?

- Find a friend in the organisation. Approach with humility and genuine interest and ask.
- Build a connection outside your line, stakeholders who will impact, find out their experiences, where the bodies are buried.
- It is your responsibility to ensure that they know what you are doing. Give solutions, advice. It puts you on the radar as safe.
- Manage the manager. Let them know you are on their side.

What advice would you give women as they reach middle management?

- Look at the competencies above and beyond the role. Stretch yourself.
- Think and believe you can and put it into action.
- Have a willingness to learn and ask for advice.

- Give respect and acknowledgment.
- Fit in to people's timescales.

What are the most important factors when you reach the Board?

- Recognise that leaders need thanks and feedback.
- Relationships are vital. Connect outside the room and build trust.
- Be conscious of who may/may not be allies.
- Be very strong on business, e.g. finances.

What is needed to ensure more women leaders in the future?

- More role models who are not male in style, or pulling up the ladder behind them.
- Relationship building and mentoring to support people.
- Ideally a fundamental re-draw.
- Encouraging the young to see what they can do.
- Share and show it is fun.
- Spotlight women in unusual roles.

What coaching have you had?

- When she became Director, as it was a big transition – needed to understand board antics, unpick the drama, find important people, pick opportunities.

When would you most have valued coaching?

- Mid point of career when entering first supervisory role and at seminal points of career transition.

What would be the most significant areas for coaching?

- Reflection time.
- Challenge – why not?
- The rules of the game – what's allowed.
- Reinforcement of own choices.
- Confidence to go for the next job.

Coaching implications

This impressive group of women are working from the inside to change a man's world into something a little fairer. They all emphasised staying female, prizing and valuing specific female attributes that are often underplayed in male-designed and dominated institutions. Specific needs are:

- Accessible, even pro bono coaching for those at the leading edge of change but lacking development budgets.
- Opportunities for reflection and sounding out of ideas.
- Encouragement to get where you are going faster.

Marketing and PR professionals

14. Norma

Tell me about yourself

Having worked as a Head of Marketing and then Head of Policy Development and Public Affairs in the tourism and hospitality sectors, she more recently became a communications consultant. This was a conscious decision taking business commitments and family responsibilities into account.

What has been important to you as a woman in your career?

Women are products of their backgrounds and expectations. As she came from a traditional Asian background, not much was expected of her. Her mother and sisters didn't work and the setting was almost Victorian. Only her latent instincts led her to want to pursue a career. She had a need to prove herself to two older, very bright brothers but discovered that you didn't need to do what men did to be a success. As a result there was no benchmarking. She was in a different field.

What difference has it made being a woman?

She used to think you had to work very hard to overcome barriers but realised that you could also stand out and be more exceptional. She used to believe that women had to grow balls to succeed. This was hard for her to relate to. Found it worked better to seem non-threatening, i.e. not to grow balls but tentacles! As a woman, she found she could be nurturing and as a result get to the parts that men couldn't. Women have the freedom to ask things that men would find embarrassing and need to use that skill to gain advantages through their communication.

What has contributed to your success so far?

- Being a really good listener.
- Wanting to deliver.
- Having a firm grounding in corporate structures and processes.
- Not being judgmental.
- Her openness to peacemaking and compromise.
- Developing solutions with integrity.
- Having a personal touch.
- Seeing people as humans first.
- Learning to deal with a range of people.

What would have been useful in your career?

- Good mentors who were both benevolent and highly professional.
- Female bosses who could have shown the way.
- People having expectations of her.

What advice would you give young women starting out in their careers?

- Go into a structured workplace and learn the discipline.
- Learn how to think.
- Learn everything you can about your speciality.
- Align with positive people who bring you up with them. Avoid the toxic.
- Have a hinterland, e.g. hobbies or home life.

What advice would you give women as they reach middle management?

- Be happy living with your choices.
- Provide a role model – today young women only seem to have WAGs to emulate!

What are the most important factors when you reach the Board?

- Create stability.
- Set a good example.
- Be a mentor.

What is needed to ensure more women leaders in the future?

- More facilitators who will give women a leg up.
- Help through the politics, especially at the top.
- Opportunities for professional development.
- Exposure to the brightest and the best.

What coaching have you had?

- Business strategies which led to good focus.
- How to approach clients.
- How to make the most of yourself and situations.

When would you most have valued coaching?

- When she made a big mistake over a job offer.

What would be the most significant areas for coaching?

- Operational in all the functional areas in order to be good at the job.
- Unlocking limiting beliefs and preconceived notions.
- Confidence.

Coaching implications

- Need to address, challenge and overcome cultural stereotypes that could block success.

• Finding inspiring role models may be even more difficult for minority women.

Implications of the interviews when Coaching Women to Lead

Conducting these interviews was a wonderful experience. All the women were forthright and opinionated. They were all very different. They had many different views and many ideas in common. As one woman put it, 'men are more homogeneous, women are so diverse'. It takes a much greater number of them to get a groundswell going. The very wide range of experiences and opinions means that it can be lonely for women, even if they are not alone in the organisation they may not have many kindred spirits. Hence, the need to find role models, mentors and establish networks as all these help to build confidence in line with women's ability.

These women were all passionate about what they did and pursued their careers and lives with drive, determination and hard work. Physical and emotional resilience was seen as vital to success and sanity.

They were from a range of cultural backgrounds and a number of different nationalities. Some had not married or established a life partner, others had decided not to have children or it just hadn't happened, the rest had varying numbers of children from one to five, several also had children with special needs. One or two felt their job could not be done if they had children, not a decision many men have to take, and at this stage in their careers some were having second thoughts and regrets. We failed to ask about that other great caring role – looking after ageing relatives and several of these women are just approaching that stage, often soon after they have seen their children off into further education or their working lives. With an ageing population this will become an increasing issue for senior women and of course for senior men.

However, issues of confidence and self-belief emerged with a depressing consistency. Despite great achievements and even a forbidding public demeanour, women were still racked by doubt about whether they were 'good enough', with a variable impact on their behaviour and career progression. Good female role models had been few and far between. They often deemed the ones they had encountered as 'scary women'.

Some of the implications for coaching women to lead:

- Women experience the world of work and organisations very differently from men.
- Every woman is very different from the next one. There is no 'one size fits all' coaching prescription.
- Coaches need to approach women with an awareness of what it is like to be female in a male-designed model organisation.
- Women will encounter much unconscious gender bias. They need to be aware of this, deal with their own emotional reactions and behave in ways that will lead them to success where they can use the opportunity to change the system. Going in blind is not an option.
- Women, more than men, can feel very lonely and unsure of who they can trust, as they are still likely to be in a small minority. Coaches can offer the opportunity for reflection and a trustworthy relationship where they can test out strategies and behaviours.
- Women sometimes struggle to find an authentic voice and make choices that fit with their values. They feel they either have to sell out or get out. Coaches have a role in testing alternative solutions with their women clients.
- Women need to learn how to be excellent role models to more junior women in the organisation and in society.

Coaching women to lead – a systematic approach to coaching women for success

Chapters 4 and 5 give clear indications from our research of what women felt had contributed to their success and what were the most important areas for their development. They told us that a combination of the following factors had been critical:

- Determination to succeed, involving long hours, hard work and delivery.
- Resilience and the ability to bounce back fast from adversity.
- Accepting all challenges and taking all opportunities offered.
- Relationship, influencing and communication skills.
- Combined focus and multitasking.
- Curiosity, willingness to learn and continuing education.
- Understanding corporate structures and processes.
- Flexibility in self and organisation.
- Balancing work with enormous demands of life outside work.
- Finding something you enjoy and are good at.

Some of these characteristics are gender neutral and can be covered in most good coaching interventions; others are women-specific but again can be addressed using general coaching techniques. Some areas however are specific to women and require a different approach. Here is our list of specific intervention areas for coaching women to lead.

- Confidence, from a woman's perspective.
- Building active, supportive networks.
- Looking for role models.
- Balancing home and work life effectively.
- Becoming resilient with the capacity to bounce back from difficulties.
- Navigating the labyrinth.
- Playing with the big boys.
- Developing presence.
- Turning into a leader rather than a 'doer'.

In this chapter, our aim is to consider some of these areas of concern and examine possible coaching approaches for each. A note of caution, however – at no point should coaching become formulaic and ritually applied. Every individual coaching assignment, regardless of gender, will be unique and the needs and aspirations of each coaching client must be carefully considered and managed. On the other hand, it is important to consider these areas and, where relevant, address them. While considering the coaching of women in this book, it should be noted that many men have problems with these issues too and that techniques and approaches can be more widely adapted and applied. In the past, one focus of coaching seems to have been to encourage women to be more like men – to be more analytical, competitive and confrontational. This may enable them to fit in to the organisation while they stay there but may lead to such a sense of being inauthentic that they feel they have no choice but to leave. Here are some of the essentials for coaching women.

1. Confidence – yes, you can!

The issue

Confidence was seen as an almost universal need amongst women. Scratch the surface of some very successful, and often daunting, women and you will find a yawning confidence gap. It is manifest in various, sometimes destructive, ways which may make women appear less predictable or logical than men. While covering for insufficient confidence, women may come across as aggressive, self-effacing or unapproachable. They routinely hold back from applying for new jobs, asking for better pay and conditions or being in line for new experiences until they are almost 100 per cent sure that they have what it takes. Men, in contrast, are more likely to put themselves forward when they have perhaps 40 per cent of what the job requires, having either the confidence or the bravado to know they can learn the rest on the job. Women may also overcompensate by micromanaging, by working excessively hard or by being racked with doubts about their right to be where they are. The word 'confidence' is used fairly indiscriminately and has been an issue for a long time. Cicero remarked, 'Confidence is that feeling by which the mind embarks in great and honourable courses with a sure hope and trust in itself'. Psychologists describe confidence in the following ways:

- *Self-efficacy*: this is defined as belief in your ability to successfully perform a specific behaviour or set of behaviours required to obtain a certain outcome (Bandura, 1977). It is a specific self-perception, and has been referred to as a situationally specific self-confidence (Feltz, 1988) as it varies according to context.
- *Perceived competence*: defined as the perception that one has the ability to master a task resulting from cumulative interactions with the environment (Nicholls, 1984). It is considered a more general self-perception than self-efficacy.
- *Confidence*: is thus an overarching concept, defined as the firmness or strength of one's belief regarding both efficacy and competence (Bandura, 1997).

Professor Rosabeth Moss Kanter (2004) of Harvard Business School says 'Confidence consists of positive expectations of favourable outcomes'. Her work builds on research by Martin Seligman about the correlation between success and a positive, optimistic explanatory style.

Psychologists have of late taken issue with what is seen as a primarily North American focus on building self-esteem and avoiding failure at all costs. What we have seen in our survey is a lack of real, solid self-belief despite manifestations of confident-looking behaviour. There is a case for working on both – ensuring that women have a strong, realistic (often better than they think) sense of their abilities and outward behaviours that illustrate their strengths effectively.

Ideally, confidence is developed early in life as a child discovers her abilities, masters new tasks and constructs a sound, positive view of her strengths through reinforcement and success. Each new experience should be approached with a sense of curiosity and add to a sound self-view and a solid set of beliefs about herself. However, for most people growing up, confidence is much more hit and miss. The lottery of innate temperament, combined with wide ranges of variably effective parenting styles is then followed by the erratic process of feedback and reward that occurs in the world of school and then work. Few people, however successful, have developed consistently strong confidence.

Confidence, like the emerging seedling, requires the correct circumstances to flourish. Too much light or too little, sufficient water and nutrition or momentary neglect all have a dramatic effect on the growth and resilience of the young plant. Even much later, conditions will determine the robustness and form of the plant. Those fortunate to have all the conditions for confidence met early in life are still vulnerable to the icy blasts of life and reality at later stages. Building confidence is an on-going task.

What accounts for the difference in confidence between the genders? Research from the 1990s (Sadker and Sadker, 1994) demonstrated that there was still a considerable gender bias in the way that boys and girls were treated in the classroom. While girls would wait patiently with their hands up to answer questions, boys would shout out and receive attention. Girls were praised for being good and neat, while boys were rewarded for being active and speaking out. For boys, bad behaviour is almost an asset. For girls, it is a character defect.

Many classroom studies still show that boys are attended too much more in class, often for disruptive behaviour. They are also given more praise and positive feedback while girls receive more criticism or just acceptance of their work.

Since that time, girls' academic results have kept improving and drawing ahead of boys' but the socialisation impact of this gender bias has a major impact when women find themselves in the organisation. They are prone to work steadily and wait for their eventual reward. This can be a limitation in the corporate world.

The coaching approach

There are two levels on which to consider confidence:

- inner belief and a strong sense of self-efficacy and competence; and
- outward manifestation of a confident demeanour and behaviour.

Here we will consider interventions to build inner belief and confidence. Although there are many potential approaches, here are some foundations:

- knowing your strengths;
- developing a constructive explanatory style;
- acting with confidence.

Knowing your strengths

Many women are very well-versed in their weaknesses. They know exactly what they cannot do or what they feel they have not mastered yet. Essential to a growth of confidence is a sense of where your talents lie and what your real strengths are. Positive Psychology would argue that understanding your strengths and then playing to them in every situation, leads to a sense of engagement and in turn to a sense of satisfaction with work and life.

Coaching technique: Me at My Very Best

1. Ask your coaching client to first think back and find a situation where she believes she was performing at her very best and then to write about it in an essay of around 300 words, focusing especially on her part in the story.
2. Ask her to read it to you while you note all the strengths you can see she demonstrated.

3. Before you share your list with her, ask her to consider what strengths she was using.
4. Check that she has covered all the strengths you found.
5. Consider how these strengths are fundamental to her.
6. Ask her to consider how she might use these strengths more in some of the difficult situations she faces.

Explanatory style

In Table 6.1 you can see that a confident woman will use an internal attribution for successes, recognising that hard work, talent or determination won the day. She is also more likely to recognise the role of external factors in her failures, i.e. circumstances were against her. The less confident woman will often have an explanatory style that is the complete reverse, attributing success to luck and failure to her own weaknesses.

Acting with confidence

Many women need to adopt the famous phrase 'fake it till you make it'. All too often women will be unsure of their entitlement to promotion, advancement and even coaching. A woman came recently to discuss coaching and said that if she were fortunate to get the promotion she was hoping for then she would be quite happy to forgo a raise to pay for the coaching as she knew it would be expensive. Her boss

Table 6.1 Explanatory styles of confident and less confident women

	Confident woman	Less confident woman
	Internal	*External*
When something good happens	I worked hard I am talented I can do my job well	I was lucky It can't have been that hard Anyone could have done it
	External	*Internal*
When something bad happens	It was a tough assignment The market was against me	It's all my fault I'm not good enough

(female) was furious at this suggestion because of course it was a sound business decision to offer the coaching to make the transition to a new senior job and it demonstrated how out of kilter this younger woman's view of herself was. A man in the same position would be unlikely to make the same mistake in interpretation. He would feel a more automatic entitlement.

There are many novel situations in which women find themselves and may need to demonstrate greater confidence than they feel. It might be useful in coaching to help them recognise that many men would put themselves forward in situations when they only have some of the knowledge required and to rehearse with them how they might take a similar risk.

Example – Jane

Our client Jane had been very successful by all standards. She had made it to the Board but became very anxious about speaking out and giving her opinion. She just didn't have the confidence to believe that she had something to contribute. It started to become a self-fulfilling prophecy as she volunteered less in board meetings and started to become peripheral in decision making. When examining her levels of confidence it became apparent that her opinion of herself was not consistent with her achievements. Nothing she did was that special in her opinion. Anyone could have done the same – so far, so modest. It was time to challenge her explanatory style with a series of questions, bearing in mind that a strong, supportive and respectful coaching relationship had already been established and that the coach knew she was robust enough to take it. Here's how the conversation went:

Coach: You say that anyone could have done what you have. Perhaps that is true but let's just go over the facts. You were top of the class throughout school – how many other people have done that?

Jane: Well, yes I did do well at school but there wasn't that much competition as it was not a very academic school.

Coach:	So despite the fact that the school was not very academic, you did extremely well?
Jane:	Well I didn't really fit in. I never belonged so I just got on with my work. I didn't do anything special.
Coach:	So – as a result of your hard work, you had outstanding results? How many people get the grades that you got?
Jane:	Well I guess not so many but they probably could if they just applied themselves a bit more. I'm not that special.
Coach:	You don't feel you are necessarily special but you do have a tendency to set yourself tough goals, to work very hard and to achieve outstanding results?
Jane:	I suppose so.
Coach:	Your hard work and results won you a place at Oxford? How many people manage that?
Jane:	Well I suppose not that many.
Coach:	You got a first class honours degree. I imagine you might think 'anyone can do that, can't they? . . . But they didn't, did they? So what was it about you that made this possible?
Jane:	Well I do apply myself. I work hard. I do my preparation. I always try to do my best.
Coach:	And I guess we can take it for granted that you are quite bright? So, what does this tell you about your ability to contribute to the board?
Jane:	I should do as I always do and prepare well and work hard. I probably do have at least the same intelligence as the other directors.

What became apparent was that Jane's explanatory style was seriously skewed. When people are low in confidence you will often discover a negative or pessimistic explanatory style.

One caution, however, sometimes you will encounter over weaning self-confidence where denial of any responsibility for mistakes is clearly verging on the deluded. This requires some challenge and reality testing. Much more common in women is the under-recognition of strengths and talents that contribute to success.

2. Developing powerful networks – you are not alone

The issue

Many women can feel pretty lonely in their professional role, especially as they see their female peers disappear from organisational life and they find themselves outside some of the traditional male networks. One of the problems under-lying this issue is the tendency of women to work hard and to have other demanding responsibilities at home. As a result they did not always feel they could dedicate time to building their careers through networking. If they weren't actually working, then they believed they should be at home with the children. This is another example of the need to recognise and deal with potentially self-limiting beliefs about what you need to do to proceed in your career and about how to justify the way you balance the many demands on your time.

One senior lawyer we interviewed maintained her biggest regret was not learning golf at an early stage of her career, while several other younger women were currently learning. They insisted that it didn't matter how well you played, you had such novelty value as the lone woman on the course that you had plenty of opportunity to make good business and organisational contacts.

The coaching approach

Aspects of networking to review with your client:

- Meeting new people.
- Making a good impression.
- Building networks.
- Maintaining contacts.
- Serving others.
- Making requests of contacts.

However, before embarking on any of these aspects it is important to double check women's attitudes to network-ing and good networkers. Table 6.2 summarises some of the beliefs that people often hold about networking and some of the alternative interpretations that emerge when clients are

Table 6.2 Challenging thinking about networking

Damaging worries	Alternative thoughts
What if I don't know anyone?	I'll make new contacts
I may not have anything in common with them	It will be stimulating to meet different people
I won't be able to break into groups and I'll end up alone	So I can try them all rather than being stuck with the one group
They may not be interested in me	I have good stories to tell
I may not be interested in them	I'll learn something from them
How can I know who is worth speaking to?	You never know where a conversation will take you
Waste of time – I have work to do	This is an integral part of my work

asked questions such as 'What might be another way of thinking about this?' and 'How might a confident networker regard this?'

Another important question to ask is: 'What springs to mind when you think about someone who is a good networker?' Here are some of the knee-jerk reactions that may emerge:

- extrovert
- showy
- sales people
- superficial
- not in our line of work
- they use people
- not serious
- social butterflies.

If your client holds these beliefs then she is likely to sabotage her own networking attempts. Explore how she does perceive herself and how she can play to her strengths when meeting new people. She might say she sees herself as:

- a serious professional;
- a trusted advisor;
- someone who builds good relationships over time;
- socially polite – I don't butt in;

- focused on the real work;
- not a raconteur/bonne vivante!

Coaching can then focus on the accuracy of the self-perception, the skills that need to be acquired and how your client can be authentic in the manner in which she comes across. Coaching questions might include:

- How do you like to relate to people?
- What is your authentic style?
- What have you got that people need to know about?
- How compelling is your story?

Each of these would enable her to define her preferred behavioural style, plan how she would approach networking events and prepare and practise for the event. Essential networking skills to review are:

- Getting the conversation started – brainstorm techniques such as asking open questions.
- Being fascinated – explore listening style, attentiveness and empathy.
- Making an impact – practise the 'elevator pitch' or 40-word introduction (challenge modest, low-confidence styles).
- Breaking into groups – examine any tendency to hold back from joining established groups.
- Moving away – good manners, over-politeness can make someone feel as if they have a foot nailed to the floor. Contemplate and rehearse acceptable ways of breaking away in order to meet new people.

Once the fundamental skills are in place, coaching can turn to planning and preparation for making the right connections. Clients may need to research who they need to meet and where they would be most likely to encounter them, so that they can plan targeted networking efforts. Time after all will always be at a premium for most women and networking events can feel wasteful if 'good' contacts are not made. It is important, however, to remind clients that some relationships will be slow burners and will not produce results for a long time but as you never know when you are 'entertaining angels unaware'. It is often worth persevering with relationships that are not immediately productive.

Once contacts are made then good networkers tend to be very consistent in keeping in touch. They rarely leave relationships to chance but build good databases, use diary reminders to keep in contact on a regular basis. Good networkers also tend to be generous with their time and attention. They send thank you notes, or books and articles in which people expressed an interest. Coaches need to work with clients to find ways of investing in relationships so that later there will be some good will to draw on and a supportive and beneficial relationship to enjoy.

This is an area which women do not always prioritise. Yet our interviews and quantitative research both demonstrate this to be a vital aspect of success.

Example – Annabel

Annabel had concentrated on her career, served her time and put in the work. She was successful but becoming increasingly isolated in the organisation. Her tendency was to get her head down and get on with the real work, which was invariably excellent. She was turning into a good leader and her direct reports thought highly of her. Yet the senior partners rarely had a chance to see her in action and few of them really knew her. As a result, she was often overlooked for consideration.

Promotion to the next level required attending networking events with clients, as well as with more senior members of the firm. Annabel felt uncomfortable and out of her depth. She resented the time it would take out of her already jam-packed schedule. Her parents were older and beginning to become frail. It was important to her that she spent time with them as often as she could. Coaching allowed specific issues to be raised:

* pressing demands on time;
* low prioritising of networking;
* lack of networking skills.

Given Annabel's competence and success, her lack of confidence in networking was difficult for her colleagues to understand. It emerged that Annabel considered herself extremely competent at getting the work done – either herself or through her team – but did not consider herself skilled in the professional communication that she felt was required for the type of events. As a consequence she had been avoiding engaging in networking activities and as she was ambitious knew it was also damaging her potential.

It also emerged from coaching that her isolation was a problem. As women had fallen away from the organisation her original support system had disappeared. She had tried a few women's networking events without finding the right one. She felt people were only there to sell to each other or to make friends, neither of which activity was relevant to her. So, coaching focused on defining what she was looking for and how she could explore a range of networking opportunities, which might meet her needs. It proved vital to coach her in networking communication techniques as she tended to either freeze as a wallflower or to bombard people with the technical details she knew and loved.

3. Finding role models and mentors – footsteps in the snow

The issue

Many of the women we spoke to had suffered from a lack of a range of female role models, or even female colleagues in their working lives. There may have been a token woman somewhere but often she was not someone women felt they wanted to emulate. As has emerged repeatedly in this book, women are not homogeneous and may need an even wider pool of role models than men.

Given the general dearth of likely candidates, women may need to become quite creative in their search, going beyond the walls of their organisation. They may turn to role models in films, literature and management books; they may need to select components from a range of women and model their own Bride of Frankenstein version of what they admire and what can inspire them. Above all they need the confidence to pursue real women when they encounter them and ask for their help, opinion, insight and inspiration.

Here is a real-life example of a role model in action:

At a recent conference for women Mary Robinson, the former Irish President, was speaking. She came across as a delightful, gracious woman. She described the fact that she was asked to speak at many conferences and had decided that she would never accept where she was the only woman. She tells organisers this sadly and offers them a shortlist of excellent women speakers. Amazingly the line up changes rapidly to include other women – the organisers have just never noticed the lack of them before. Many of the women commented that day about what a role model she was for elegant, gracious, feminine but effective behaviour, which produced change without drama.

Similarly, possible mentors may not just appear but may need to be searched for, asked for and approached directly.

The coaching approach

Coaching can give women the opportunity to reflect on how they develop their own style of leadership, drawing from examples they have seen around them or encountered in literature. It can be useful to use a series of leaders of both sexes as a stimulant to discussion about good leadership. You might want to try taking a selection of photographs of leaders, brainstorming the qualities they possess and the ones which fit with a leadership style the women would want to espouse. Bit by bit it is possible to construct an Identi-Kit picture of leadership qualities. Often these are described in reverent, unattainable terms at first but the more they are explored the more feasible it can be to emulate or adapt.

Also vital is to explore the strengths of the individual woman and consider with her whether she needs a role model in her own likeness or as an alter ego who may challenge her to be bigger, braver or more subtle in her behaviours.

Example – Carol

Working in finance, Carol found that she had very little contact with other women. When the subject was explored, at least part of her search for a role model seemed to be about determining who she wanted to be but she had no one to compare with.

Here is how the coaching conversation went:

Who is your hero/heroine?   Well, when I was very little I loved Wonder Woman!

What was it about her that appealed to you then?   She seemed so competent and resourceful, yet human. She could be very female but also very strong. And had great legs!

What appeals to you about that combination of attributes?   Well, I think it sums up what women are mainly like (except for the legs) but I don't see much of it around.

What do you see?   I do find it very off putting when women emulate men. It seems quite phony and I feel resentful. I don't want to be forced to act like that but it feels like there is no choice.

No choice?   Well, obviously you can behave differently but it might make you stand out.

How do you feel about standing out?   Hmm, I was brought up to think it was a bad thing and then found it is quite hard to do in a work environment where men always speak louder than you do.

Have you encountered any women who do stand out in ways you admire?   Yes, I suppose so when I go to events I sometimes see more senior women from other firms. Some of them come across really well.

In what ways could they be role models for you?   I could watch them carefully, analyse what they do, how they handle themselves and see which behaviours really work.

What aspects of their style would you like to try?   The kind of poise they have. They don't get flustered. They take their time. They have a really delightful way with people, have retained their sense of humour and can handle nonsense with a light touch.

How would it feel to have one of them as your mentor?   That would be terrific. I would love to know how they have done it.

How can you go about making that happen? Goodness! I never thought of just asking them ... I just assumed they would be too busy. Well, what's the worst that can happen?

4. Balancing career and family – a woman's place is ... in the wrong?

The issue

Hardly a week passes without a newspaper article laying blame for the end of civilisation, as we know it, at the feet of women: if you work, you damage your children; if you stay home, you limit their intelligence and you waste your talent and training.

Much of what is printed is badly substantiated and is contradicted in articles the following week. Too late as the damage has been done! It all plays into women's readiness to feel guilty whatever they do. It also feeds the need for women to justify the way they are tackling life by criticising the way that other women have chosen to live their lives – pitting career women against homemakers rather than respecting the continuum of choices women, as opposed to men, have to make.

In our interviews we had a cross section of working women. Some had chosen not to marry, some had chosen to marry but not have children, others had just not had children and others had up to five children! At the other end of the life cycle, these women were, to varying degrees, facing the challenge of older family members becoming more frail. Because many of these women had had their children a little later and because of their social and geographical mobility, family members were able to offer little support with childcare during critical times.

So there is little or no homogeneity among women while men have a more direct passage through life. Coaching needs to take account of two major themes:

- the many decisions to be made as women crochet together a care system that enables them to feel confident about their children's or elders' care; and
- the emotional toll women face.

A client recently spoke about her newborn – a surprise baby born when she was in her early 40s. From the start of her pregnancy it had been decided that her partner would stay at home with the baby while she returned to work and the better job. It was the right decision, she had no doubt, but no one had warned her of the fact that, 'I feel like my heart is being ripped out through my chest every day when I leave my baby behind. Nobody warned me and I can't let people know that at work.' Of course, she was not alone in this experience. It just felt that way. It is as if it is a woman's guilty little secret that she adores her child and wants to provide the best care. At this stage mothers often feel separation anxiety much more than their well-cared-for children. Fathers may feel pain at leaving their children behind in the morning but they never face society's censure. Even if both parents have careers, we know that the balance of caring and organising usually falls to the woman. As one man very honestly admitted, 'I don't even think about my children while I am at work, because I have complete trust in my wife's ability to make everything right for them'.

When talking about balance there is rarely any space left for the activities that women find replenishing. Their tendency to multitask, to work to high standards, to expect the best of themselves all mean that they sell themselves short on the activities that give them time to restore their energy, reflect on their successes and plan for their own needs as well as others.

One of our clients is an equity partner in a forward thinking law firm. She has worked a four-day week for years and was one of the first part-time partners appointed. Now that her child is at school, she could work full time but has chosen to keep that one day every week for visiting the gym, playing tennis and pursuing intellectual development. Many women envy her but it has taken determination and reflection to understand that this is the most satisfying way for her to work. That firm now has another part-time partner on the Board – a man, inspired by her example to put more balance in his life. The work still gets done . . .

When people talk about work–life balance it is often seen as quite a rigid 50:50 split, giving equal attention to different aspects at all times, instead of seeing a more fluid process throughout life where the ratio will alter at different ages and stages of life and career. One big problem is that women often feel that unless they give all to each part of their lives then they are under performing and short changing people. Women sometimes find the 'good enough' solution difficult to accept in their own lives. For women balance needs to be an explicit three-way split between work, family and self that is actively managed.

The coaching approach

There is no one solution for women in managing career and family. Thankfully, good coaches are never prescriptive. Exploration around values will reveal very different standards and motivation for women. It is important to help women to think about a full life, i.e. what are all the aspects that contribute to their sense of satisfaction.

Coaching technique: The My Life Mind Map

It may seem an exercise in paradoxical thinking to try to put even more into an overstretched existence but this exercise is about getting priorities established.

Ask your client to create a mind map with the word 'Me' at the centre. Each arm as shown in Figure 6.1 should then depict each of the important aspects of her life as she sees it, e.g. home, family, friends, holidays, career. Keep going until everything is covered.

Ask her to then brainstorm the important aspects of each of those – the deal breakers, without which life is less satisfying. By now you will have a picture of what the full life looks like to her.

The next step is to look for the priorities and the balance that would work best for her. This will be a combination of

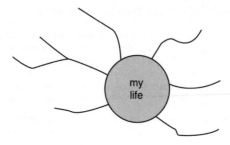

Figure 6.1 The life mind map

intellectual, emotional and behavioural challenges as illustrated in Table 6.3.

As several of the women who were interviewed stated, 'You can have it all, but maybe not all at the same time!' Men rarely have to make choices based on altruistic beliefs such as, 'My children/ageing relatives need me'. These choices usually entail sacrifice of personal goals for at least a period of time. Such decisions are never easy and if not clearly thought through can lead to underlying resentments and an embittering sense of loss. At least one woman we interviewed admitted that she had believed it impossible to have children and pursue her career. She now thought differently . . . but it was too late.

Coaching is vital for women at stages of their lives where they need to make very big decisions. The decisions will always be hard but at least the assurance that they have considered all options will enable women to engage constructively in their lives. Women may become so locked into narrow beliefs about how a career must be pursued that it is vital through coaching to help them step back and brainstorm alternative creative ways of working.

The next step may then be to coach them to present new solutions to the organisation which are based on good business sense rather than doing women a favour. Job sharing came about through women developing a solution that suited them but also gave the organisation tremendous value for money. It is after all only a brief period in most women's lives that requires thought and flexibility.

Table 6.3 Good coaching questions to find balance

Question	Responses signalling problem areas/source of possible solutions:
What impact are you having on the different parts of your life?	Nothing is ever good enough
What impact is life having on you?	I am exhausted and grumpy I don't have time to do things I enjoy
What do you think about your own performance in each of these areas?	I am never good enough I can't waste time building my career
How do you feel about work and home	I feel guilty about everything I feel angry about the lack of support
What impact does that have on your behaviour?	I can come across as quite aggressive with people who don't seem to take things as seriously as I do I retreat into working harder and harder and miss out on the 'boys' club' activities like the pub and entertainment events
What would balance look like to you?	I would feel I had done a good job on both fronts and I would have a little time for myself to read and relax
How can you achieve that? Who can help?	Well, I maybe need to be a bit more relaxed about getting help with the chores I hate, e.g. hire a cleaner or personal trainer, negotiate free time with my partner, allow myself a night out every week – sometimes to network and sometimes to party

Example – Pauline

She found the re-entry after giving birth to her first child challenging but doable. Five years later after the birth of her second, it wasn't going as well. She now had two children of disparate ages and needs. Her first child was entering the reception class and life was further disrupted by the sleepless nights of this more demanding second baby. At work she was determined to prove how well she was handling her role. She appreciated the way her company had been supportive but as she was the only part-time worker at her level she felt exposed to scrutiny. Combined with being dog-tired, she felt constantly guilty that she was less than perfect on all fronts. She wasn't really enjoying life much at this point.

We carried out the *My Life Mindmap* to explore everything that made her life worth living but currently felt like a burden. In reflecting about the different areas, Pauline recognised how much satisfaction she gained from specific activities at work, from her partner and children and from her personal life. Once these were elicited, it was possible to see how they interacted and how they all needed to be prioritised. As a result many of the less significant areas could be streamlined, delegated or put on the back burner.

It was also the time to discuss her career timeline. Some important questions were:

- How do you see your career developing?
- What do you feel you will be most needed in your children's lives?
- What are your immediate goals in all these areas?
- How will life change over the next 5, 10 years?
- What style of working would suit you best at each stage?

As a result of this in-depth consideration, Pauline began to realise that she might allow herself not to pursue her career with her previous urgency until her younger child was more settled and perhaps even at nursery. By taking the pressure off herself for a relatively brief period she began to see that she was doing an excellent job; that she did not need to do it all to prove her competence; that she could delegate many tasks in all aspects of her life; and that finding time to keep both her mind and body replenished was vital.

5. Resilience and the capacity to bounce back from difficulties

The issue

> 'When the going gets tough, the tough get going.'
> 'If you can't stand the heat, get out of the kitchen.'

These are some of the sayings bandied about in organisations. Every woman interviewed mentioned the need to deal with constant pressure, long hours and daily challenges. Then unlike many men, they often had to go home and do it all over again. As a result, it would be easy to become exhausted and to feel compelled to reconsider career goals. Yet, some people thrive in these conditions while others languish. Women especially need to be resilient in order to keep functioning at the peak of their ability. People talk a lot about balance and often feel frustrated at the lack of any in their lives. More useful is the concept of having the full life. Many women want to work hard and have a good and satisfying life but need to understand and bolster the support systems that keep them functioning well. This involves keeping the mind and body fit and ready for action in even the busiest of times, ensuring performance is maintained at the highest levels.

Coaching can make participants aware of their own constructive and destructive approaches to resilience. It will enable them to build a personal model for living adaptive, healthy and productive working lives.

The coaching approach

Psychologists have long studied the development or absence of resilience and the consequent impact on health and well being. Resilience is the process by which an individual functions well under pressure, recovers quickly from adversity and develops adaptive coping behaviours.

We all have three inter-related sources of resilience as illustrated in Figure 6.2.

- Cognitive resilience: coaching for positive and constructive thinking.
- Emotional resilience: coaching constructive handling of emotions.
- Behavioural resilience: coaching for effective actions.

By coaching to strengthen all three of these areas, resilience will be built on solid foundations.

Coaching for cognitive resilience

- *Beliefs* – build constructive positive beliefs about self and the world. Challenge negative beliefs.
- *Thinking styles* – recognise any unproductive negative thinking styles e.g. catastrophising, ignoring the positive, all-or-nothing thinking.
- *Optimism* – work hard to build optimism by coaching your client to look for the positive in everything she does.
- *Problem solving* – widen her repertoire. Positive emotions help get rid of tunnel vision.
- *Knowing your place* – coach her to recognise the strengths she brings to any situation and enable her to believe she can add value.

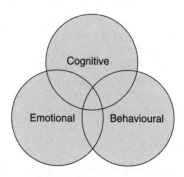

Figure 6.2 Three sources of resilience

Coaching for emotional resilience

- *Self-awareness* – coach her to develop insight into her own emotional style and behaviour.
- *Emotional literacy* – encourage her to practise reading and recognising emotions in others.
- *Relationship skills* – work on developing ways of handling others elegantly.

Coaching for behavioural resilience

- *Self-medicating* – in times of challenge avoid junk food or other quick fixes like caffeine or alcohol. Ensure that she medicates through good nutrition, rest and exercise.
- *Building support systems* – coach her to find ways of actively engaging in supportive networks.
- *Playing to your strengths* – work to develop her confidence in who she is and how she can use her strengths to get her through.

Researching her own sources of resilience

We found that women have a tendency to try to do it all themselves, to be brave and soldier on and sometimes to become martyred to their own cause. It did not come easily to many of the women we interviewed to ask for help. Many had had to overcome guilt about employing cleaners, nannies, personal trainers etc. yet they all acknowledged that most successful men had a home Executive Assistant in the shape of their wife even if that wife had her own career to pursue.

So, it is particularly relevant to coach women to establish the right support system for their needs. For instance, one woman may need help with her children and another with ageing relations. The wheel in Figure 6.3 can be used to explore in coaching every aspect of life where your women clients can build the right strengths and support to deal with the challenges of work most effectively.

Example – Barbara

The markets were down. Everyone was working night and day with little letup. Barbara was getting to work as early

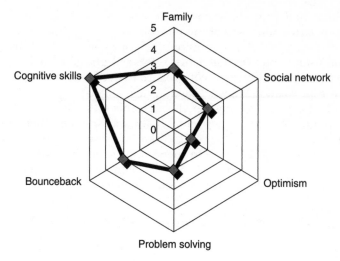

Figure 6.3 **Probing for aspects of resilience**

as she could and returning home late at night. She didn't feel she could afford time to stop working so ate convenience food in front of her computer. She took taxis to and from the station at each end of the day. Most days she couldn't tell you what the weather had been like outside as she hadn't raised her head. She wasn't sleeping at night as thoughts swirled round her head and she felt constantly guilty that she wasn't seeing much of her teenage children or her husband. On bad days she worried that she was heading for divorce as her husband didn't seem to believe she had little choice about her workload. She felt coaching was an indulgence she could not afford the time for but her boss insisted.

What was clear was that this pressure of work was going to continue unabated for some time as her organisation fought to find a way out of the worst of its problems so the main issues seemed to be keeping Barbara strong enough to get through and finding ways of ensuring her important relationships stayed strong.

Coaching focused initially on good habits such as walking from work back to the station at the end of the day. She found that in the heavy traffic she was almost as fast as a taxi and that she enjoyed the exercise as it gave her a chance to undo some of the tensions of the day. She decided also to take a brief 15 minute lunch of salad and fresh fruit and found that she felt more refreshed and clearer in her thinking on her return. With regard to her family, she carved out time to sit down with each in turn and ask for their help and support in getting her through this difficult time. They were all relieved as they had felt she was shutting them out of her life and volunteered to take over responsibilities for her as long as she aimed to spend some good time with them every week. She felt both relieved and replenished by the interventions she made as a result of coaching.

6. Navigating the labyrinth – finding the thread

The issue

There is a lot of glass around! The term *glass ceiling*, coined in 1986 by Hymowitz and Schellhardt in the *Wall Street Journal* to describe an invisible barrier which prevented women from succeeding, has more recently been superseded by new terms. The concept of a ceiling as a non-permeable barrier did not work in the light of the small number of women who did make it through to the top. It also implied that men and women had equal opportunities to that point and also that such a barrier was invisible until you met it rather than present at every stage of a woman's career. Furthermore, it bred a range of solutions which while excellent in themselves might not tackle the fundamental problem of a dwindling pipeline of talent. In 2007b, Ryan and Haslam introduced the concept of a *glass cliff*, arguing that women were more likely to occupy precarious positions when they reached the top with a much higher risk of failure. This is based on empirical evidence that the reins are only given to women and other minorities when everything else has failed. This has strong coaching implications, but we prefer the more recent concept of a *glass labyrinth* because it applies to all women in a career, not just to the few who make it to the very top. The labyrinth was developed by Eagly and Carli in 2007. It works better as a metaphor and lends itself to a coaching approach for women. Not all labyrinths have the threat of a minotaur at the centre but they do offer a challenging route through many difficulties to a potentially attainable goal. The labyrinth for women involves:

• prejudices that favour men and penalise women – such as unfair evaluation bias in favour of men at every level where gender is known;
• resistance to women's leadership style – transformational leadership is known to be more effective, yet men's more traditional transactional leadership style is preferred; and
• balancing work and family responsibilities – women are judged on their responsibilities while men's family role is overlooked.

There are implications for legal, political and organisational change in order to reduce the unfairness of the system. Women cannot wait for that to happen. So what we address here is the way that women need to behave to navigate the existing labyrinth.

The coaching approach

There are clear implications for dealing with the greater complexity required when coaching women. Women must first realise that they have entered a labyrinth and then decide at each stage of their career how to deal with it. There are no specific *tools* for dealing with the labyrinth, but a detailed awareness of the journey and of the obstacles along the way is essential:

• *Recognising the nature of the labyrinth* – many women still start off in their careers believing they are on an even playing field. It can be a shock to discover they are not even in the park or playing the same game. Coaching may need to focus on discovering the complexity of their situation, dealing with the emotional reaction that evokes and then building a constructive repertoire of behaviours. We know that on the one hand 'out-manning the men' tends to lead to criticism from both men and women. On the other hand, a more female style of leadership behaviour, which can be highly effective, is rejected mainly because a traditional male leadership style has been in the ascendancy for many years – whether it produces results or not. So women have a minefield to navigate on top of developing a personal, authentic and effective leadership voice.

- *Preparing for the journey* – how can women prepare themselves for the challenges? What do they need to have in place, e.g. education, mentors, networks, etc?
- *Finding your way through* – women are likely to face more important choices which will affect the rest of their careers. They need to start well in advance of certain choice points to ensure that they align their careers as positively as they can. Persistence, stamina and resilience will play an enormous part. Coaching may need to focus on the development and maintenance of these characteristics at each stage of the career journey.
- *Overcoming obstacles* – coaching has a real part to play when women feel they have slammed into a brick wall or a dead end. Coaching may need to focus on creative problem solving and the seeking of novel solutions.
- *Changing track* – for many women their career will not follow a straight, clear line. There will be times when they need to consider taking a diversion, a change of track or even a U-turn in order to approach the goal they desire.
- *Taking a bird's eye view* – by rising above the labyrinth the pattern becomes clearer and potentially productive pathways possible. Being able to see the pitfalls and take preparatory action in advance, women may have a greater chance of building the successful careers they seek.

Many of the other topics in this chapter will also be extremely relevant to women's passage through the labyrinth, e.g. developing presence and staying resilient in adversity.

Example – Kate

Kate was ambitious and hard working. She had a lot of confidence in her own ability and had always held her own in the situations she encountered. However, lately she was feeling quite disillusioned. She had begun to see cracks in the system, which seemed quite unfair. Recently she had noticed that some of her male peers were being given opportunities and that she had been overlooked. When she took this up with her boss, she was told that her personal style was a bit aggressive. When she reviewed the conversations she felt sure that she had been professional and assertive and realised that it felt like there were different standards for the men and women in the organisation. One of her bosses, when recounting interviews he conducted, told her that, 'I expect men to blag. I would do it too and I sort of give them points for trying it but when I catch a woman doing the same I mark her down as it just isn't what women do.' Kate was furious when first seen in coaching. She realised that men were allowed to be ambitious, forceful and controlling while women were meant to be influential, empowering and caring, yet the leadership style that was most respected was the former even though the latter could be more effective. She felt she just couldn't get it right whatever she did and that she was now resentful and stuck in this stage of her career. There were many areas to tackle in coaching. Here are a few:

- *Reflecting on what had happened* – Kate was experiencing a massive emotional reaction to her experiences. Bottling up her rage only meant that it leaked out in small angry spurts at inappropriate moments. Exploring what this unfairness meant to her allowed Kate to recognise and calibrate the level of feelings she experienced. She could then consider how they could be either expressed or dealt with. Only when she had the emotions under some control, could she move on.

- *Finding another way* – Kate could go blindly banging her head against a brick wall (because it ought to work) or try to find an alternative opening. Coaching needed to address whether this was the end of the road for this firm, whether she felt she could find ways through to personal advancement, whether she believed the organisation would change for the better at any point and whether she wanted to be part of it. Her first instinct had been to get out, 'shake the dust off her feet' and start somewhere new.

- *Overcoming current obstacles* – as Kate decided she would make a concerted attempt to get through the system ('Don't get mad, get even!', she said) before deciding the organisation was a lost cause, coaching involved brainstorming the different people and the many ways she could influence to achieve her goals of being appreciated and perceived as a talented individual with a good future. She had to challenge her belief that she should be able to do it all herself and, as a result, sought out the support of a more senior male colleague who had previously admired her work. By asking him to mentor her, she gave herself a better chance of discovering the inner track. She would have been incapable of taking this step if she had still harboured her earlier fury.
- *Taking the bird's eye view* – with both the coaching and mentoring she was able to rise above the current annoying circumstances and her strongly held beliefs that 'It shouldn't be like this' in order to look at how she might need to position herself and organise the timing of major events in her life (relationships, family) in order to ensure her success. Then by achieving her personal goals she felt strongly that she would be in a position to influence for change in the ways that women were perceived.

7. Playing the game with the big boys

The issue

Girls do better than boys at both school and university and enter working life on a par with their male counterparts. They then start to disappear from corporate life. We know that girls are still differentially rewarded for being good with others, for working hard and for making good grades. By the time they enter work, women have been trained to expect to be recognised for making A grades and working hard. It strikes many as deeply unfair that the rules are then changed. It seems that the attention seeking/rule breaking so typical of boys at school return to dominate the culture of most companies. Quite a few of the women we spoke to were mildly dismissive and disparaging about the politics and lobbying for attention that went on – 'boys and their games' they said. Yet if women persist in their deeply held belief that good work alone will pay off they may miss the opportunity to showcase that same work, raise their profile and be seen by the people who can influence their careers.

The coaching approach

Different women will react differently to these asymmetric rules between boys and girls, ranging from paralysing anger to low energy and helplessness. Again, there are no specific techniques but a need for putting first things first: before starting work on changing behaviour, the coach must spend a considerable amount of time understanding the thought processes and emotions of their clients – we refer you to Chapter 7 for detailed models.

Example – Jean

She was angry. People kept being credited for work that she had done. Then she had been acting up to the next role but discovered the post had already been given to a male colleague. They hadn't even put her on the list of possible candidates. She made a fuss about the process and there was much embarrassment. She felt they made a show of considering for the job but she still didn't get it. At that point she made up her mind to leave the organisation as she felt it did not value her. That was when she was offered a coach.

Table 6.4 summarises our approach.

Table 6.4 Summary of our coaching approach for Jean

Stage 1	*Reviewing facts and emotional state*	She felt angry and upset that they had overlooked her contribution
		She realised that they took her for granted as always working very hard.
		She came to see that they had not registered that she was interested in the job.

(Continued Overleaf)

Table 6.4 Continued.

Stage 2	*Checking, testing and restating beliefs*	Jean felt very strongly that 'by their fruits ye shall know them' i.e. results should speak for themselves
		Jean felt guilty that she was not 'working' when she was spending time influencing others on her behalf.
		She reconsidered these beliefs and recognised that she had a responsibility to get that message across to those who could influence her career.
Stage 3	*Deciding on a strategic action plan to raise her profile*	Jean had done amazing work but received little credit for it. She was never going to be comfortable boasting about it, so we explored ways of using her influence, finding mentors and advocates and asking for their help (something she was usually too independent to try).
Stage 4	*Changing her demeanour and developing gravitas and presence*	Jean sometimes fluctuated between diffidence and aggression. We worked on her body language, voice and her professional preparation for showcasing her talents at meetings.
Stage 5	*Preparing for interviews*	As a result of her new impact on people Jean was put into the running for several jobs with different career opportunities. We worked with her to discover her preference and to prepare for the interviews.
Stage 6	*First 100 days*	Once Jean was successful at moving up to the next big job, coaching focused on hitting the ground running, making an impact on her team who were mainly older men who had been in the department a long time.

8. Developing presence

The issue

Presence and gravitas are essential aspects of senior management for both men and women. Experienced coaches know that there is a set of skills, beliefs and attitudes that can be taught and rehearsed until they become second nature. However, as usual, it is a bit more complicated for women. Because of the dearth of women at more senior levels in organisations, they are likely to be either under scrutiny or overlooked altogether. What they wear, how they look, the way they sound, how they carry themselves are all at least as important as what they say. In essence coaching needs to focus on three aspects:

- Appearance
- Impactful behaviour
- Confident presentation.

Coaching for appearance

As one of our interviewees commented, senior women are not always a good advert or role model as they often look frazzled and as if they aren't enjoying it much. We have had female clients referred where some of the feedback concerned aspects of their grooming – not enough time spent at the hairdresser or having their nails done. It is rare to have comparable comments about men 'letting themselves go'.

Classically, women have often gone the route of emulating men, donning a pin-striped trouser suit in a dark colour and avoiding manifestations of femininity lest they should be judged lightweight or draw attention to their differences. Many of the women we interviewed while recognising a need to look professional wanted to reject this idea of 'pretending to be smaller, unthreatening versions of men' and wanted to be able to combine some femininity with business-like professionalism. Some of this comes from the clothes, hair, make up and accessories and some from the way women handle themselves. Whatever grooming a woman takes part in, the really critical issue is about managing other people's perception and ensuring that she is making the right impact for the setting.

There is much more pressure on women than on men to appear slim, fit, well groomed, well rested, well dressed – even when life is at its most hectic. There is no right answer or single way to do this and the regimented style of business-women of the past has squashed some of the aspects of their personality as they attempted to clone themselves. They may need some encouragement to consider how they construct their own personal 'brand message' in terms of a congruous presentation style. It is not unusual for our clients to have a role model in this area. The coach should draw out aspects that can be tried out. Some of our clients 'dress up' for coaching sessions until they find a style that is personal, congruent and comfortable.

Coaching for impactful behaviour

As we have known for a long time, both body language and voice represent the essential component of our communications. Men by their very size can easily make a greater impact than women. When coaching, it is important to examine the way that the woman:

- *Enters a room* – does she look a bit apologetic, kick the door open like she owns the joint or walk in looking like she has a very real role to play and contribution to make?
- *Takes up space* – ask any woman about commuting and they will complain about men sitting legs wide, arms akimbo, with their paper at full stretch while the women squash up. This sense of men taking up space is seen in the boardroom too. Work with women clients to see how they can make their presence a little bigger and more impactful but always in a constructive fashion.
- *Uses her voice* – women complain about people ignoring their ideas, yet lauding someone else who makes the point slightly later in the conversation. It is almost as if women's voices are in a key that men just cannot register – like those frequencies only dogs or teenagers can hear! Check that women are on the one hand not holding back tenta-tively or going to the other extreme of being strident

or snide in a 'does anyone ever listen to me?' sort of way. They may need to practise raising their voice while lowering their tone to avoid being seen as aggressive. It is also important to avoid ending up with an unnatural sounding Margaret Thatcher type of voice. It may be important to refer at this stage to a well-qualified voice coach.

- *Makes a point at a meeting* – using voice and forceful body language, women may still need to be coached to be 'impolite' on occasions and butt in to make a point rather than waiting in a polite but frustrated fashion. They also need to be prepared to be less than 100 per cent right and so may need to think of ways to frame points as questions or opinions.

- *Makes her presence felt in general* – 'putting yourself forward' at least in Britain was for a long time frowned on in girls. Times have changed and many young women become adept from schooldays at putting themselves across confidently. However, many of the women already in post were brought up to be more self-effacing.

Working hard is not enough. Women need to be encouraged to find ways of being seen by a wide range of people who can recognise that they have something worthwhile to say. Coaches can achieve a lot by working with women on finding and expanding these opportunities.

Coaching for impactful presentation

Presentation training and coaching are essential to both men and women. Specific aspects for women include:

- *Not setting themselves up for failure* – we have seen countless examples where a young woman executive has been put in the line of fire by an overworked boss: 'you'll do this presentation, it will be a good opportunity'. Pretty much each time we have analysed reasons behind a less than 100 per cent successful delivery, we have recognised an impossible task in terms of preparation time, content familiarity or experience dealing with a large/senior audience. Women should jump at the opportunity to gain exposure, but on their own terms: through training coaching, rehearsing, etc.

- *Finding her own tone* – many of our clients initially thought they would have to emulate men's style of jokes and sports metaphors. Rehearsing both the structure and the narrative of an important presentation is a worthy coaching exercise.
- *Getting honest feedback on her style* – many women have a distorted perception of their presentation style (too modest, or having no awareness of their voice). Coaches can rarely be flies on the wall when their clients are presenting. Obtaining tapes of public speeches or organising 360° feedback to cover presentations is extremely powerful.

Generally, it will be valuable in coaching to role-play each of these or other situations generated through the coaching process until a more productive style has been achieved. The coach also has an important role to play in preparing the terrain: dealing with values, beliefs and any psychological barriers to authentic performance. Coaching should always check the need to be authentic and genuine but as women become more confident, they also become more themselves.

Example 1 – Eva

A client, working in the electrical industry, spoke of how difficult it was being in such a traditionally male industry as a foreign (American), mixed-race (father was from Hawaii), short (she was 4'11") woman. It would have been easy to be empathic and spend some time on these issues. As it happens we had had the chance to observe her as she came into the room for her first session. She stopped at the PA (not her own) who was sitting outside and in almost a whisper had extremely apologetically with many 'If it isn't too much trouble', 'Can I possibly ask a favour?', 'So sorry to bother you' and many 'Thank you's', with the most subservient body language, had asked the young woman to hold her calls! Having observed this demeanour it was possible to coach her on developing a quiet, firm, assertive but gracious style while making the best use of the height she did have. We developed the image of a small dog that can run rings around a bigger more lumbering breed. We worked on her posture and on more confident, firmer gestures while also building up her knowledge of her strengths and her confidence in her contribution.

Example 2 – Alice

Alice had been very successful in her HR career and was appointed Director. This necessitated speaking at the global conference to a large audience. For some this would be their first encounter with her and she felt this could make or break her career and also her success in the role. She was extremely anxious and tense when presenting. Her voice became quite strained and high when she was tense and she looked very young for her age. Coaching focused on what it would take for her to have gravitas in this situation and as a result the coaching goals were multi layered. Coaches worked with her:

• on understanding the beliefs that were causing the anxiety – 'I could really mess up, look like an idiot and never work in this field again' was gradually through challenging and rebuilding a belief system translated into 'this is a great challenge but I know my stuff, I am excited about my role and I am going to prepare well';
• on breathing and relaxation techniques to both prepare for the stage and to enable her to use her voice in a variety of ways – modulating her tones, emphasising her words, varying the pace, etc. in a way which prevented her from sounding breathless and girly; and
• on delivering a serious, strategic and challenging message.

When reviewing her experiences in coaching Alice was thrilled as she knew that she got her message across and was seen as a heavyweight in her field by the audience.

9. Developing into a leader rather than always 'doing'

As repeated throughout the book, with so few senior women to model themselves on or to look to for encouragement or inspiration, women may not be inspired to become leaders and may not be well equipped to demonstrate leadership ability. Many of the available models of leadership are a predominantly male construct, rooted in male designed and run organisational theories and approaches. As women do not identify with the paternalistic, autocratic, heroic leadership styles they have often observed, they may consider themselves unlikely to succeed and even less likely to enjoy a leadership position. In the next chapter you will find what we consider a more balanced view of leadership which is also more likely to appeal to women.

Women are also often described as lacking certain essential leadership traits. If women have any one curse it could be said to be their talent for multitasking. Men, in contrast have a capacity for a narrower focus. The words, 'Here, give it to me. I'll do it', may sound the death knell in women's advancement as they are seen as good implementers but less as good leaders. They need to learn to delegate effectively to extend their influence and to make time to think strategically and see the big picture.

Some of the aspects for consideration when coaching women on leadership are how to enable them to develop a strong, authentic point of view and how to avoid becoming a male management clone while pursuing success.

Women are often held back by ambivalence about ambition. While they certainly want to get on and will be highly resentful about being overlooked, they may not pursue success as ruthlessly as their male counterparts. They eschew what they consider 'male games' and often leave themselves out of the circles of influence that would guarantee advancement. They may not pursue promotion with determination but will rather expect to be given opportunities once they have proved themselves, overlooking the fact that many male bosses fail to spot ambition in women as it looks very different from ambition in men.

The coaching approach

There are many aspects of leadership at which a woman may need to work conscientiously. Here is a small selection of important aspects.

Thinking about leadership

All coaching inevitably commences with taking stock, understanding what you want to achieve and examining the efficacy of your beliefs and behaviours. For women, it is often important to push beyond the surface to examine beliefs that may restrict the ability to step up to leadership.

Table 6.5 Eliciting beliefs about leadership

'Some coaching questions'	Possible responses
What are the characteristics of good leaders?	Decisive, inspirational, strategic . . .
How do you compare?	Well . . . not sure I measure up.
What strengths do you have?	I get things done. I reach my goals. I work very hard. I form good relationships.
How can you deploy those in this new setting?	Well I would really want to achieve any goals I set . . .
Where might they get you into trouble?	I set very high standards and can't bear people falling short. The risk is I will keep getting dragged down to the detail.
What other strengths can you use to avoid that?	I am good at clear communication and motivating others. I can see how I could achieve a lot more working through other people and encouraging them to encourage others.
What will it take for you to become a good leader?	As far as the people side of it is concerned, I am a good leader already. I think I have to realise that thinking is actually work and that I have to set aside time to read up, study the business and think through some of the big picture stuff.
What else could you do to further that?	I think it would be useful to do some formal leadership training and then have more coaching to make sure I lock the behaviours in.

Coaching can help women to formulate clear goals, test their beliefs and emotions concerning them and set in train the behaviours that will lead to success. They can enjoy the support and encouragement that coaching offers. It is in the coaching relationship that they can check out models of leadership and develop their thinking about authentic and professional leadership behaviour. Key areas of development for women are likely to include learning to think strategically and learning to be a co-ordinator of others' efforts rather than constantly an implementer (in Belbin terminology).

Stopping micromanaging

Ask any woman to write down every thing she has to do today and the list probably starts very early in the morning and goes on till very late. You may want to limit this exercise to just the working day with men but with women sometimes the whole of their life is worth considering.

The Alien Abduction exercise

Imagine, if you will, that you are unexpectedly airlifted by aliens. Nothing unpleasant will happen but you will be absent from work for the next 3 months.

List everything your job entails. Then for each task decide:

Who could do it now, if necessary?	Highlight in green
Who could do it, if they were coached?	Highlight in yellow
What can you alone do?	Highlight in red

What else should you be doing?

How would you like to develop your job once you return to find all these other tasks taken care of?

This exercise encourages some creative thinking and also some decisions about whether you *have to* or *want to* do certain things. The next step is to then delegate and coach the team to take over the bulk of what you have previously been doing, leaving you free to coach and reinforce good behaviours while spending more time on the big picture.

Building personal strategic effectiveness

Because of this tendency to become involved in the detail, women often need to develop their strategic competence to become the most effective leaders.

Good strategic leaders build their own models of their business and their industry and take the time in their busy schedule to think about possible scenarios and their consequences. They engage others to join them at being future-oriented and then place some long-term bets and work flexibly to make them happen.

Here is an important question to ask about the way a woman is working:

How much time do you spend in a typical day . . .

- Doing the day job/extinguishing fires?
- Managing people?
- Managing stakeholders?
- Thinking about the future/developing strategy?

Coaches need to help women to develop as strategic leaders who have, above all, an ability to rise above the daily noise of their job to think about the future using a mix of analysis and creativity to constantly challenge their own assumptions about the sources of competitive advantage

Engaging her intellect

As we have seen elsewhere in this book, women may neglect their own development due to perceived and actual lack of time, responsibilities as a carer or concentration on the job in hand. It may fall to the coach to challenge women clients to consider how they can most efficiently keep themselves abreast of current thinking, asking perhaps:

- *What should you be reading?*
- *Who should you be talking/listening to?*
- *What media should you follow?*
- *What courses do you need to take to stay sharp in your thinking?*

And the rest . . .

The eight preceding sections of this chapter might all be involved in coaching women to lead; when women are promoted, they often question whether they are good enough. They may lack the networks where they can compare circumstances or emotions and they may find role models thin on the ground. They are still balancing several aspects of their lives with resilience while navigating the labyrinth. Now they really are playing with the big boys and need all the presence they can get as they work to become true leaders.

Example – Wilma

Wilma had spent some time in coaching considering her beliefs, values and goals. She had been extremely happy performing at her current level but was unsure of whether she really wanted or was able to pursue her career further. She talked about the fact that her mortgage would be paid off in six months and she might decide then to take a less demanding role. It was only when she honestly considered her options in coaching that she realised how very ambitious she was and that she needed to make that known in the organisation. In coaching, she rehearsed for conversations with the Talent Board. As a result she could clearly articulate what she wanted next in her career.

She was offered an opportunity to take responsibility for a strategic change programme. Although it certainly seemed to meet the career goals she was seeking there were a couple of aspects on which she would have had to compromise. As a result of the coaching, she decided she wanted more and pursued a more exciting opportunity instead. As a result, she was offered the chance to design and lead a new part of the business from inception through to delivery, with the career progression and the Board accountabilities she had been working and aspiring towards. She attributed her success in getting this promotion to the clarity she had acquired through the first phase of coaching. She now admitted that she was equally ecstatic and terrified about the new role. Like many women she was prepared to admit to doubts about her ability to step up to the challenge. So the next phase of coaching then concentrated on her key issues – conceiving a strategic focus, building an excellent well-motivated team, running motivational meetings and empowering her direct reports while ensuring that high quality was maintained. In other words she worked on becoming a Balanced Leader.

Implications when Coaching Women to Lead

- There is no one recipe for success.
- There are specific areas which are likely to be of greater importance to women than to men.
- A dilemma exists: do you coach women to fit male designed and dominated organisations or do you work with them to be authentic and successful in their own way?
- Women have to consider their caring roles at the same time as their leadership desires.

What makes a strong leader? A model for women's leadership development

There are thousands of books and articles published every year on leadership but it remains an elusive concept. Our perspective, after 60 years of combined coaching and leadership development experience, is that leadership education is a lifelong journey: some travel quickly and some travel slowly; some focus on gaining concepts, others prefer experiential learning; some learn by themselves, others need to practise their ideas with others. Coaching is an important component of this education.

So in this chapter we re-examine what makes a good leader and how coaching can help. Our perspective is that there is a core set of skills and aptitudes that should be central to every leader's development. We expand on our ITEA model first presented in *Essential Business Coaching* and enrich it with recent research that looks at eight long-term characteristics for emerging and confirmed leaders. We call our new model the *Balanced Leader* and for each characteristic we point out any gender-specific issue and the coaching approach to deal with it. This can be seen as a long-term roadmap for all leaders to follow. According to our research, Balanced Leaders are:

- visible
- resilient
- strategic
- emotional
- decisive
- intellectual

- behavioural
- meaningful.

The ITEA model of change

We have refined our approach to coaching models based on coaching hundreds of senior executives and concluded that a cognitive-behavioural approach is what works best in business: it addresses the concerns of highly rational managers as well as engaging those – such as entrepreneurs – who are less receptive to an intellectual approach. It generates new behaviours, creating a tipping point when they will become installed as habits. ITEA stands for:

- Impact
- Thought
- Emotion
- Action.

Impact

What impact do you have in the situation in question and what impact are these events having on you? Without this self-awareness, change and development cannot happen. Once clients decide that their actions are not necessarily achieving the desired impact on circumstances they can seek to change their thinking and behaviours accordingly. This stage is always the catalyst for change.

Thought

'There's nothing good or bad but thinking makes it so', as Shakespeare's Hamlet says. Recognising and changing how clients interpret events, by assessing how they filter them through beliefs, values and previous experiences determines their chance of success. Change must occur at these deeper levels to be authentic and sustainable.

Emotion

This is often the overlooked piece of the puzzle. If emotions are a closed book to clients then they do not harness the strongest possible motivation in themselves and others. The research shows that emotional intelligence correlates highly with success. Yet many people have an underdeveloped emotional literacy. They have never learned to measure and classify emotions accurately. As a result, they can be at the mercy of their own emotions and remain amateurs in their dealings with others.

Action

Translating all that into sustainable, constructive behaviour change is the ultimate culmination of coaching. Sometimes there may just be better ways of doing things that people have ever thought of. The whole process of coaching allows clients to stand back from their normal life and achieve a sense of perspective not available in the daily turmoil. It is only once destructive assumptions and negative emotions have been cleared that new varieties of creative thinking and problem solving can enable the client to move out of tunnel vision and experiment with new ways of doing things. By adding a range of professionally honed techniques to their armoury, clients' results improve exponentially.

Illustration: the ITEA model in action

A client, bright, successful and tipped as 'high potential' by her direct boss, was seen by colleagues in other functions and divisions as 'a bit of a lightweight'. Her way of dealing with others was both unsophisticated and she was generally punching below her weight outside her area of expertise.

The first stages of the coaching made her aware of these opinions through a number of interviews. She was initially mortified by the findings and her first reaction was to become paralysed by the enormity of the mountain to climb. How could she engage people who were so different from her? (They were mostly engineers.) We started by analysing what *impact* she had on others and what impact others were having on her. At a superficial level, she was still dressing like a junior employee and her voice rose to a high pitch each time she tensed up. She came across as very awkward and at times dismissive of other people. Her presentations lacked the hard data that colleagues required for decision making. When she had to attend multidisciplinary meetings, she found it difficult to get her point across and felt people did not listen to her with the professional respect she deserved. When her beliefs were explored, it became clear that she made assumptions about people's attitudes and was highly judgmental about colleagues from different, more analytical, backgrounds.

At first she believed that changing her style would be inauthentic and inappropriate. We challenged her **thoughts** by requiring her to build up evidence for and against her assumptions rather than blindly believing them to be true – for example, regarding how people absorbed information and how people could be persuaded of ideas. In this way, she learned to change some of her damaging thought patterns, e.g. people were rude not to listen to her. By testing her own assumptions and finding a new set of beliefs, she approached this work with professional skill and broadened her understanding of to impart ideas.

Her **emotions** included discomfort in a range of situations away from the world she knew best. By recognising that many of these feelings were engendered by her negative assumptions and a lack of flexibility, she could change the whole process and take **action** in a very different way, by developing greater sophistication in her communication style with others, dressing to create the impression she desired and becoming more confident and human in her relationships.

Coaching enabled her to see that by asking questions and listening attentively she could create opportunities to bring people around to her view of the issues and the potential solutions. As a result she began to play a much greater part in the team and earned the respect of her colleagues. By embedding these changes so thoroughly in her own distinct personality and core values, the sustainability of the change has been guaranteed.

This process is cyclical. With each new topic raised or experience reviewed the coach is likely to have to work back through each of the areas.

The Balanced Leader model of leadership development

The ITEA model, especially when augmented with the latest findings in Positive Psychology, is at the core of what a leader should be. In addition, we formulated a series of 'level 2' competencies, to be developed as leaders move from 'emerging' to 'confirmed'. We refined these competencies over five years and tested our assumptions via a recent survey of 127 leaders and senior HR executives (see *The All-Weather Leader*; Provencher, 2007). This confirmed our assumption that all eight of our competencies were statistically significant in developing strong leaders. We now look at these in turn and comment for each of them where there is a need for a women-specific coaching intervention.

The visible leader

> *'Balanced Leaders are grounded, demonstrating presence and gravitas, as well as inspiring others – both internally and externally.'*

When asking existing partners in professional services firms the one leadership quality they find hardest to teach, they invariably list gravitas first. When asking middle-management teams what is the most important quality they expect from their leaders, inspiration is what is often missing.

Gravitas and visibility are typically acquired over time but this acquisition can be accelerated through specific interventions combining psychology and theatre techniques, including creative writing and improvisation. Coaching issues more likely to be relevant to women include:

Physical presence

All other things being equal (e.g. size, confidence) many women tend to speak with a smaller and or higher voice when exposed to stressful public speaking situations. Voice and posture coaching can make a huge difference to the perceived impact of interventions.

Difficulty putting one's self forward

We have already seen in Chapter 6 that women are more focused on the doing than on the bragging. This can be a problem in a company where the unwritten rules of recognition include making one's views explicit, both in everyday meetings and during conferences or other high visibility events.

Different ways of displaying ambition

Blame it on the testosterone, but women tend to be more subtle in displaying their ambition. The main danger here is that they are simply not seen by their male colleagues who are more used to territory-circling rituals.

In the last two cases training and rehearsing what will often be uncomfortable situations works well.

The resilient leader

> 'They know that they are running a marathon, not a sprint. So they are physically fit to lead, emotionally resilient and socially secure.'

We have explained in Chapter 6 the three sources of resilience. The dangers of stress include a sudden drop in performance, tunnel vision and entering a vicious circle of isolation and cutting one's self off from the very sources of resilience. Whereas many men work themselves into the ground, they usually have a good awareness of what is wearing them down and what to do about it. Women tend to do better on the social aspects of resilience, provided that they maintain their network. When they get really busy however, they may no longer have the time to access their external network and the internal one may not be robust enough. Women-specific coaching issues around resilience include:

Reluctance to ask for help

For many women the issue is that they do a day's work and then get home to do another day's work and are reluctant to ask for help. Most men are pretty good at getting help both at work (PA) and at home (wife). For each woman with serious home backup for example we can cite dozens who skimp on support. This is due to a variable combination of guilt (their mother did without), the habit of putting one's self last and a simple lack of awareness of the need. A coaching intervention in this area should obviously focus on the cognitive aspects of the situation, drawing as many relevant external comparisons as possible.

The need for perfection

We return to the theme of perfection or failure: men are typically more comfortable with the concept of 'good enough'. If a woman must do something 100 per cent right or perceive herself a failure, then she is removing a number of safety valves from her busy diary. This can be wearing over time. Coaching in the area of knowing what to 'let go' as responsibilities increase can be very useful.

The strategic leader

'They are obviously future-oriented; they have well developed models about their business and their industry and do not confuse budgets with long-term thinking. They are also very good at making strategies happen.'

Most men have a clear understanding that, for their career to progress they will need to become more strategic – whatever that may mean. As a result, they tend to articulate views about the future of the industry or long-term developments at their company fairly early in their career and not necessarily when in possession of full information. The extent of this is driven largely by cultural factors in each industry.

Our observation is that there is no difference in strategic capability between men and women, but that women tend not to 'own' the issue as early as men in their career. This can be driven by many possible factors: from the reluctance to take sides in the absence of sufficient information, to being too busy delivering to actually spend 'non-productive' time thinking about the big picture. Coaching in this area should focus not only on approaches to strategic thinking but also, more broadly, on how emerging women leaders choose to spend their working time; there is a parallel between this and the need to invest in networking as seen in other chapters.

The emotional leader

'Balanced Leaders know how to manage both their own emotions as well as those of their teams. They are subtle motivators.'

This is clearly an area where women are usually better equipped than men: their emotional literacy is key in running things smoothly, managing teams and generally getting things done with minimum pain and maximum efficiency. However, many men do not value EI because they don't 'get it'. Women therefore need to showcase the relevance of their skill.

Drilling deeper in terms of emotional competence, women score higher than men on self-awareness; however they do not necessarily know what to do with it. EI coaching should initially focus on self-management.

The decisive leader

'They know how to balance science and intuition, have well-honed models for risk-taking, articulate their decisions clearly and delegate work with the right scope and trust.'

There is a perception among men that women leaders are risk-averse. As illustrated in Chapter 5, they are merely risk aware and tend to make smaller losses and gains than their more testosterone-influenced colleagues. The importance of this perception will vary tremendously with the local culture. Again, it is a case of advertising their special skills and putting themselves forward, especially in board situations where 'group-think' on big decisions is always a possibility.

At a more specific level, there is a perception that the proportion of women with a scientific training is lower than that of men (in non-scientific industries), so they may be less attracted to complex quantitative decision-making tools. Hard data are hard to find but it is worth pointing out that, according to the Higher Education Statistics Agency (2008/09), exactly 50 per cent of science graduates are women. Assuming however that there is indeed a science bias, then women should be particularly well suited to modern approaches to complex decision making such as Scenario Planning where a combination of intuition and commonsense are particularly relevant.

Finally, women – like men – usually benefit from coaching on best practice in delegation. Whereas men do not delegate because they do not easily trust others to be as competent as they are, women will hold back delegation because of the need to get things absolutely 100 per cent right every time. As a consequence their schedules will get overly busy and the thinking time for big decisions may be squeezed out.

The intellectual leader

'They take responsibility for their development. They understand that there is no "silver bullet" approach to leadership. They constantly refine their understanding of the world and never become prisoners of the received wisdom of their industry or function.'

The value of education and an intellectual approach to management varies more by culture than by sex. For instance in the UK, most managers are suspicious of over-conceptual approaches and a lot of management education is case-based (inductive) as opposed to model-based (deductive). Even in the USA where university is highly regarded, successful dropouts are celebrated.

With this in mind, are there any differences between men and women? Our view is that women will tend to skimp on development programmes, especially those that require nights away from home (although those who do attend feel like they are on holiday!). Many women simply do not have the time to invest in personal development while holding two full-time jobs. Development was analysed as an important strategy in Chapter 4 but the analysis between what women actually do and what they wish they had done indicates a measure of regret. This was confirmed by answers to open questions.

Also, as men tend to attend more learning and development events, we have again a case of men subtly pulling away from women by building a better CV and as well as networking at these events. The coaching intervention is therefore to help women invest their 'spare' time wisely. The role of the coach is also to emphasise the worthiness of investing in learning capital.

Regarding the informal aspect of developing an intellectual perspective of leadership (i.e. having more than one model of leadership, understanding that there is no single silver bullet), most women have a head start, being more detached from an expected model of behaviour (and leadership); those who are mothers also have a serious grounding in 'behavioural flexibility'.

The behavioural leader

'They test ideas and install those that they find useful as new habits in a systematic and disciplined way. They are creative in getting support for those new habits. They ensure that their teams do not stay stuck at the conceptual level but that agreed decisions are actually practised day-in, day-out.'

The picture for women in this area is mixed: on the one hand our experience tells us that more women score high on the 'steadiness' dimension than men – most tend to get on with it and are not easily derailed. This is exactly the right approach to install and practise new habits, as well as ensuring that promises made in meetings are kept.

However, a side effect of being a high 'S' (steadiness) is to accumulate resentment vis-à-vis those who don't pull their weight and bear a grudge. In behavioural terms, it means that many women easily swing from passivity to aggression. This is neither predictable nor explicable by men working with them. Coaching may need to focus on enabling women to find constructive, professional ways of expressing their reactions and needs to their male colleagues rather than repressing what might be a very relevant reaction.

The meaningful leader

> *'Balanced Leaders find meaning in their daily and long-term actions: they really intend to change the world – in their own way. They articulate their values clearly and know how to share them with others towards a common goal. They are particularly good at negotiating phases in their career where motivation and meaning could become an issue.'*

The standard behaviour for men is to play the competitive game and to be too busy to think hard about meaning. In some respect the expectation of the man as a hunter/bread earner is their default position. Many reach a stage where they question meaning, but it is not until quite late in their career. We covered the topic in detail in *Essential Business Coaching*: 'They spent the first part of their lives training for success and the next stage working hard to achieve it. For many, the time then comes when they wonder, "Is this it?" Somehow the satisfaction they had expected is less rich than they had hoped for and does not have the power to motivate them for the next stage of their lives.'

Most women tend to find meaning much earlier in their careers: pretty much all women interviewed in Chapter 5 find their careers extremely stimulating and exciting, but they would drop them instantly if their family really needed their attention. For men – particularly those below 40 – this 'volatile liability' borders on the inexplicable. The challenge for women is therefore two-fold: how to find meaning at work, as well as at home; and how to manage men's perceptions.

The coaching intervention for meaning at work is similar to that for men in their mid-career crisis: take stock of the past, focus on signature strengths and work towards building something bigger than the day job.

The coach can also play a key role in checking that clients are not moving with haste towards an area of activity for which they are deeply unsuited: some clients of ours have initially jumped into teaching only to come out a year later for example. A coach will also be instrumental in checking beliefs about what is possible and feasible: some clients may be preventing themselves from making a success of the next stage of their lives.

Testing the evidence for their beliefs gives the opportunity to assess how achievable their goals are. Careful consideration must be given to all the factors, from financial implications to family attitudes, which must be addressed in order to make the transition. At this stage consultation with other relevant advisors such as accountants or lawyers will contribute to the efficacy of the process.

Our experience is that most clients (women and men) think about career change because they tend to reject the past as a block (*all or nothing* thinking). In many cases fine-tuning their role and making some lifestyle changes can be just as effective at finding meaning as moving to Australia or starting a commune.

Implications when Coaching Women to Lead

- General coaching interventions for core leadership development are all applicable to women leaders, specific interventions have been described in details in Chapter 6.
- Advanced leadership development requires specific interventions: in some cases women have a head start, in others they have a handicap. In most cases men will find it difficult to understand why women behave differently and coaching will need to take this into account.

How to develop a woman-friendly organisation

Corporations and government departments compete for Talent along two axes: they compete with each other, but also against other forms of occupation. Women who leave corporate environments do not simply vanish or turn into full-time mothers, even though they often seem to be air-brushed out of corporate history books. Many women are choosing to go into business for themselves or to join smaller companies simply because the corporate format is deeply out of tune with their needs and aspirations.

By now it should also be abundantly clear that organisations have very strong reasons to retain and promote women: the business case is robust (Chapter 2) and women are clamouring for it (Chapters 4 and 5). Companies can't keep ignoring half of the population much longer in times of talent scarcity. So we need corporate environments that are basically more women friendly, in a pro-active way.

We know from observing reactions to competitive pressures that companies can be extremely slow to change, particularly where there is strong history of past success – not unlike the infamous story of the frog that boils to death if the heat is raised slowly enough. The pressure to increase women's role in senior ranks has been applied very gradually. After all it is supported largely by demographics: not the fastest of change agents! Also, women are relatively new entrants into the managerial workplace, when placed in the context of agrarian, industrial and post-industrial econ-omies. In order for us to define a general change agenda, which will be supported by coaching in many organisations, we first need to take an objective look at the historical context.

The historical context

A slow start

From the onset of the industrial revolution, women were placed in low-ranked jobs, often along with children. It is the enduring image of the factory girl, replaced by the pool typist when economic activity moved from factory to office.

A career in this context had a rapid ceiling: perhaps rising to a team leader at best – by heading a team of women. While we don't believe this was intentional – more evolution of a typically paternal society – it has produced a lasting effect on our world of work today.

The situation remained more or less the same until the 1970s. Armies of secretaries and female administrators as abundantly illustrated in popular media. The film *Nine to Five* may seem quaint today, but it was only released in 1980. The social mores of the day limited women further. For example, up until the 1970s, a woman working in a bank was expected to leave when she got married.

Thirty years of evolution, not revolution

By 1974, the UK had a tiny proportion of female managers, as shown in Table 8.1. All in all only 2 per cent of

Table 8.1 Percentage of female executives in the UK by responsibility

Role	1974	2001
Director	0.6%	9.9%
Function Head	0.4%	15.8%
Department Head	2.1%	25.5%
Section Leader	2.4%	28.9%
Whole sample	*1.8%*	*24.1%*

Source: Davis and Burke, 2007; *Women in Management Worldwide*.

managerial roles were occupied by women. The comparable figure today is 24 per cent (with 11 per cent of company directors being female): a twelve-fold increase, albeit from a very low base.

The situation in the USA was a little bit different: although women already represented about 13 per cent of all managerial roles in the 1950s, the curve remained very flat until the 1970s. According to the Department of Labor, the number then doubled to 26 per cent by the late 1980s.

In the UK, changes were largely driven by law:

- The Equal Pay Act of 1970 meant that women now had to be paid at the same rate as men for doing the same job. A year later, in 1971, women earned 63 per cent of the average hourly earnings of men. By the turn of the century, it was over 80 per cent, so their level of pay is gradually creeping up.
- The Sex Discrimination Act was passed to give women equality with men. Both Acts have been amended and updated since. Interestingly, the Sex Discrimination Act also covered indirect discrimination. This has proved helpful to women (and other minority groups at work) over the decades. For instance, if a neutral employment practice has a disadvantageous effect on a particular group, for example when an employer imposes a condition which applies to all but in reality can only be met by a small group of employees – the Act is there to put an end to such practice.

Positive discrimination is not a feature of British law, unlike the USA. However, positive action is not outlawed and means companies are free to do more for under-represented groups such as women. For example, they can be encouraged to apply for jobs, companies can set targets for recruiting them at certain levels (e.g. adding women to senior management or the board of directors) and can also provide access to women for special training, which may allow them to overcome any earlier educational disadvantages, to move up the management hierarchy.

Positive action in the 1990s

The 1990s was the decade when most companies woke up to the fact they needed to do more to recruit and retain women. This was due mainly to the demographic evolution, as seen in Chapter 2. Many companies recognised they were missing out on half the population in the talent pool. Equally important, they perceived the huge talent and financial waste caused by so many promising women workers leaving around the 30-year mark. Initially, this led to the growth of women-friendly and family-orientated policies. These typically improved company maternity-leave conditions and pay, paved the way for the first paternity-leave initiatives and included different ways of working such as flexible working, part-time, term-time work and job-sharing. Attention was also paid to the life–work balance as companies recognised they needed to do more to improve the UK's long-hours culture to help family life. This has only been partially successful, as witnessed by the many stressed, over-worked people coaches see today.

While many of these policies are to be applauded – for the first time ever, companies acknowledged that they needed to offer more, to think how family life impacts working life and to understand the needs of women workers better – they did not address many of the real problems affecting women in the workplace and their woeful ability to progress through the rank to senior echelons. Women-friendly policies are, however, not just about maternity leave and flexible working – they are a lot more complex.

The real current demographics and responsibilities of senior women

Many of the standard work–life, family orientated practices that organisations offer were designed with a specific demographic in mind: married with children. For decades now, the best support programmes have been devoted to this group of employees.

For many women, this demographic is meaningless: a large proportion of highly qualified women are childless (a recent study of global companies gives the figure of 44 per cent) – this was confirmed by our interviews – including over 50 per cent of women professionals aged 28 to 40. Childlessness is a fact of life for many senior women.

In addition to this, nearly a third of highly qualified women are single, with or without children. This can have very different implications for the level of support needed.

An often overlooked issue – yet picked up in our interviews – is the high frequency of caring roles for professional women. 24 per cent of professional women off-ramp (leave their jobs temporarily) because of an elder-care crisis. If elderly family members become sick, it is far more likely that a daughter or niece will care for them than a male relative. A recent *New York Times* article (Gross, 2006) calculated that 71 per cent of those devoting 40 hours or more a week to this task are women. As Sylvia Ann Hewlett (2007) concludes in her book *Off-Ramps and On-Ramps*: 'If a talented woman is not derailed by a two-year-old at age 35, she may well be derailed by an 83-year-old at 45' (pp. 161–162). It is therefore equally appropriate to design leave/re-entry policies for this group as for mothers.

Another interesting problem affecting women, that has recently come to light, is the extra caring responsibilities expected of women from diverse ethnic backgrounds. Professionals of colour, particularly women, routinely take on responsibility for needy young people in their extended families and communities. The argument can be extended to any culture where mutual support and extended families are the norm. They are much more likely than their white colleagues to reach out and give back 'as big sisters, godparents and honorary aunts'. This affects their time and energy most of all, but is also an extra financial drain as well.

As coaches we are likely to be asked to coach more senior women (and men) in companies. Being aware of these facts and demographics affecting women at work may prove vital to coaching approaches.

Designing the women-friendly organisation

Objectives and measurement

Without quantified objectives and relevant measurement, companies will not be able to trace progress and evaluate their competitive position along the two key dimensions discussed at the beginning of this chapter.

The key metrics are straightforward for a successful women-friendly organisation – just remember the digit 3:

- at least 1/3 women in middle management (or 33.3333 per cent . . .);
- at least 3 women in the top team (senior executive team, preferably on the board).

At present a number of organisations are quite good at the measurement and reporting of gender diversity. This is typically focused on:

- recruitment (the gender balance of those recruited and the balance of those on the recruitment panel);
- induction and progression (measuring and reporting on the career development of women at various stages);
- salary differences;
- representation of women in senior roles; and
- the measurement and reporting of women's leaving rates.

This is a good start as it already allows us to create the business case for coaching described in Chapter 2. It fails however to measure the very things that tend to make a difference, for example:

- proportion of women in senior CV-building stretch jobs; or
- attendance of women at training events.

If a company for example doesn't objectively realise that few women go on to take up the tough (stretch) projects (e.g. turning around a failing business in a remote part of the world), then it can't start to design comparable challenges nearer home and more suited to a woman in her early 30s' lifestyle.

Obviously measurement cannot be dissociated from targets. For example in many professions 10 days of training per year is the norm. If Learning and Development reports that women only take, say, 30 per cent of their entitlement, then it is a clear signal to design different types of events, perhaps some closer to home or with fewer away nights. It is worth remarking that, in this specific example, we would not argue against short overnight stays as they are part of the informal networking so many women are keen to experience more of.

Process to build an authentic women-friendly organisation

It may come across as semantics, but in our experience it is essential that management be committed to building a genuinely women-friendly organisation, not simply slap on policies – no matter how good. Perhaps a metaphor would be that of a Zero Based Budget: how would you build an organisation from scratch where a woman could come to work as a woman, not just a worker?

An interesting analogy is to compare it with a disability-friendly organisation. In such an organisation, there will be ramps installed to allow those with disabilities to enter, work and do business there. While no one is suggesting women are disabled, a women-friendly organisation will provide invisible ramps so that women can realise their full career aspirations – just as men have always been able to, without even thinking about it. What is more, much research shows that if companies are already doing this, they are making themselves more accessible to other minority sectors of the population – or other sectors of the talent pool on which they may have been missing out.

The LBS/Lehman process

The Lehman Brothers Centre for Women in Business at the London Business School (LBS) in 2007 examined the practices of 61 organisations operating in 12 European countries, across a range of industries – from cars to utilities (Gratton, Kelan and Walker, 2007). LBS concluded that there are four clear interventions which companies can use to inspire women at work:

- measurement and reporting on numbers and how women progress at work;
- enabling women to be wives, mothers and carers;
- creating support networks; and
- preparing women to be leaders.

The study is careful to distinguish between aspiration/best practice and reality: sometimes the culture is working against the right decisions, a bit like those companies where it is frowned upon to take your full holiday entitlement. For instance, LBS computes that fewer than 10 per cent of women managers take up flexible working policies or job-sharing: a number well below estimated need. This is down to many factors including culture and, with only 1 senior position out of 10 occupied by a woman, that culture is largely driven by men.

Making men part of the process

A deep reconfiguration of an organisation's culture will not take place without the support of the majority. According to the US advocacy group Catalyst, bringing men into the conversation on gender diversity is essential. In a 2009 report, they describe men's positions as follows:

- In the supporting camp, one finds men who clearly see the business benefits of increased diversity, as well as men who have a strong sense of fairness. They are more likely to have personal concerns about issues of equality (they often cite struggles their wives or partners have had at work; many also worry about their daughters entering the world of work); and were more aware of gender bias at work. They are also more likely to take or demand action.
- Men who don't advocate gender diversity tend to fall into two camps: fear of losing status or being seen as part of the problem; and apathy – a sense that gender issues do not concern men. In our experience there are also a number of men who reject any form of affirmative action outright, either out of the same sense of fairness/ meritocracy or because they think 'why not me?' In both

cases they tend to think that there *is* a level playing field for women and are not yet receptive to the business arguments.

Organisations can take steps to remove these barriers and engage men in initiatives to promote gender equality by appealing to men's sense of fairness. They can provide men with women mentors, expose men to male leaders who champion inclusion and invite men into the discussion through male-only and male/female groups. Obviously this can form part of coaching conversations with men: for example, when exploring ways to increase financial performance, or gaining competitive advantage. After all, we know that most men react actively to targets, especially if they are of a competitive nature.

Content of the woman-friendly organisation

So what does the women-friendly organisation look like? From our research, to the LBS research, to conversations with organisations considered to be operating best practice, here is our wish list:

* Make the obvious work: maternity and part-time roles.
* Design appropriate support networks, especially in-house ones.
* Build stretch jobs and other pre-leadership experiences.
* Invest in coaching and mentoring early on.

Working arrangements for mothers and carers

We won't expand on these: best practice and innovative policies abound. The key challenge is likely to be cultural. For example, in the USA many clients and bosses like to 'see face', limiting the practical appeal of remote working. In the UK, law firms think that if a client is served by job-sharing Partners, somehow it is not the same as being served by a dedicated one: only a handful of firms offer part-time Equity Partner status. We have heard plenty of senior women who work a three- or four-day week explain how they cram a 60-hour week into those days.

Support networks

WFOs need to pro-actively create support networks as part of their design process. As we have seen in Chapter 4 it is an essential part of what women want. The emphasis is on *in-house* networks: women want to understand the rules of the game, the range of desirable/undesirable behaviours and the opportunity to identify firsthand potential mentors or simply like-minded colleagues. Networks also provide a voice for women feeding back to the organisation about ways of creating change at work.

Companies should focus on creating several types of networks:

- Induction networks.
- General professional networks.
- Career planning networks.

These networks are extremely popular: in the LBS sample database, 75 per cent of women participate in those that exist!

There is also a plethora of external networks of varied usefulness. One worthy of mention is the FTSE 100 cross-company mentoring programme. In this initiative, 28 of the CEOs of the FTSE 100 companies volunteered to mentor senior, high-potential women from other, non-competing organisations. Operating at the highest levels of industry in the UK, this initiative not only gives senior high-potential women visibility both inside and outside their companies, but it also provides legitimisation and role-modelling for the mentoring of women.

Stretch jobs and other pre-leadership experiences

As we have already seen, each company has its own type of CV-defining moments: key experiences in middle management that identify people 'who will go far'. Women-friendly organisations can actually do a lot to formalise these experiences and ensure that women who want to are given a fair chance to enhance their prospects (as well as monitor and report progress). The challenge is to design comparable and valid experiences for those who cannot travel in far-away countries or commit to 12 months of 80-hour work weeks.

Some have tried with success: Volvo recently made a concerted effort to bring a business-critical project to women. The You Concept Car (YCC) Project brought together a women-only team charged with designing and building a car that would appeal to women. The project team was able to secure senior sponsorship for building a concept car that would heighten Volvo's responsiveness to female customers and deliver a real impact in key markets. The learning is not about the focus of the car (it could have been a truck for that matter) but about the validity of bringing a major product to market.

Coaches have a vital role in challenging women to consider their options and in building their confidence in their strengths so that they can contemplate more challenging leadership roles.

Coaching and mentoring early on

We have seen that *Confidence* and *Role Models* are issues that are present at all stages of a woman's career. We have also seen that the early 30s is when the biggest damage is done to the women's pool of potential leaders. Women-friendly organisations offer coaching and mentoring to that age group and are creative about managing their investment. Here are some ideas:

- Make mentoring a formal responsibility of senior managers – get them to look after at least two new persons per year.
- Offer mixed programmes of one-to-one coaching, networking and topic-based seminars, for each cohort of young women managers.
- Apply Talent Management processes earlier in the case of women: offer coaching to promising women managers in their late 20s/early 30s.

A good example of a mentoring setup is Unilever: its system of formalised *reciprocal* mentoring between very senior men and women executives at least two job levels below them. Speaking with those who have taken part, the men approached it with particular ideas and mindsets about women managers, while the women have their own impressions of what it takes to do a very senior job. Interestingly, both found they changed their views once they started the reciprocal mentoring! The men began to perceive women managers in a more positive way – they also had the opportunity to work with women, a rare occurrence in many cases. As for the women, the project gave them exposure to those at the top and the ability to establish working relationships with senior men, as well as renewing their confidence. It encouraged women to consider applying for the big jobs and ensured that the men were less likely to dismiss women who applied for roles higher up the career ladder. Dell has also undertaken a mentoring initiative. Ingrid Devin, Dell's diversity manager for Europe, Middle East and Africa region, said: 'The feedback from the men was great. They realised that they have a lot to learn about the challenges that women face in the workplace, especially learning how to do the "right thing" ' (Hopkins, 2009).

Emerging topics for the women-friendly organisation

Even a well-designed and filled women-friendly organisation is not a static object: it needs to constantly monitor emerging or poorly identified subjects as any change will take some time to be put in place. Here are a few.

Engaging Generation Y women

Generation Y is made up of boys and girls born between 1983 and 2001 (definitions vary). They are sometimes called the Echo Boomers as they tend to be the children of Baby Boomers. They have always known technology, extreme communications and networking. Their attitudes to authority and leadership are different from those of current leaders. For this age group diversity is a fact of life, accepted as normal and does not need to be stressed to them. Another LBS survey – *The Reflexive Generation* (Kelan, Gratton, Mah and Walker, 2009) – shows that this generation believes there has or will be a lot of progress in relation to gender. They talk about how a gender balance is slowly being reached and how gender discrimination is no longer an issue of modern workplaces. The glass ceiling is perceived as a thing of the past and many young professionals have a firm belief that equality between men and women has been achieved and will no longer be an issue for them.

At the same time, however, young professionals admit they experience a very traditional gender culture at work – identifying that 'business is a man's world'. They also acknowledged something changes when men and women have children in their 30s, although they could not be specific. Also, issues with female role models became evident. When discussing women's networks, the assumption was that these are for older women and that older women were less willing to help other women up the career ladder. Interestingly, these responses were fairly uniform from both Generation Y males and females. On the subject of having children, most Generation Y males wanted to play a far greater role in the lives of their children and families – and overall would like to create more egalitarian patterns.

Again, this informs us when coaching this age group. It remains to be seen if Generation Y, renowned for being idealistic, will retain this level of optimism. What we do know is that diversity, including gender, is a fact of life for this generation and they will question inequality. It should also be clear to companies that they need to organise themselves for a Generation Y workforce because it will inevitably be very different to that of the Baby Boomers or even Generation X.

Treating women as individuals

The logic of the corporation is typically that of a sausage machine: design the best and most cost-effective process, then fill the funnel with as many cases as possible. However, those who have been involved in the practice of gender diversity for many years (some decades) are finding that single-issue processes are obviously good at solving part of the problem for many women, but never provide a total solution for the individual. This leads us to three key observations:

- Issuing guidelines and practices, rather than policies, may be a better way forward: it allows a certain amount of flexibility, whereas policies do not.
- The same way HR departments have been very good at spreading 'cafeteria' benefits – encouraging staff to pick from a menu up to a given monetary value, may be appropriate to women support processes.
- Moving from a logic of binary 'gates' to more of a cyclical review of potential is highly appropriate. For example, if a woman has 'missed the gate' of the stretch job early in her career but finds herself at 45 without young children and raring to progress, the system should be able to identify her and provide the right springboard. This is a situation where coaching the individual would be highly effective.

What women can do for themselves

If a woman works in a very male-orientated organisation, or at a very senior level as the only woman, she will naturally feel lonely and most probably substitute at least some of her female management skills for male ones in order to fit in. Ultimately this will have a negative effect and either lead to her leaving the organisation to join a more women-friendly one or to her subjugating her authentic self further and possibly generating long-term frustrations or stress.

One of the first things a woman can do in this situation, other than get a good coach, is to join an internal or external women's network, especially those related to her industry or profession. This will give her a social and support network in her job and build her confidence. If there is no internal network, she should seek to organise one as soon as there is any critical mass of women managers in her organisation (it doesn't need to be a large number). This will achieve most of what an external network does, but makes it more personal and targeted as it is part of the organisation in which women work; it also makes men more aware of women in the workplace. Furthermore, making it clear to men that they can take part, running meetings with speakers and inviting men along goes some way to integrating men into a woman-manager's mindset and should open their eyes to how life really is at work.

The next thing she can do is to put herself in the mindset of reaching senior roles. Only then will she be able to identify the steps required to get there, present her case convincingly and help change rules and processes along the way. For example when a senior role at oil company BP came up, two senior women who both wanted promotion but who could not work a full week due to family commitments were interested. Having met, they decided to approach HR to propose to share the role. Not only did they present a fully compelling case as to why they were the best combination to take on the role (a strong mix of management experience and complementary business and personal skills), but they also persuaded the company to make the job a six days-a-week role so that they could overlap for a day. Their proposal was accepted, despite the fact that this was in the middle of a cost savings round, and it has been running successfully since 2007. The arrangement has even survived one of the partners changing! There was a strong risk element to doing this – it is vital for women at work to feel they can take risks. Again this is not something men would debate over. They are much more likely to take risks.

Finally, in keeping with being authentic to herself, a woman can create her own authentic 'brand'. This is a very powerful way of understanding who she is, what she wants from life and from her career in particular and determining how she presents herself to others and her organisation. Spending a little time working through these questions can help her to achieve what she wants, particularly from her career. It will give her the additional confidence and help her to build a vision so that she can take risks and challenge her own mindset – both of which will help her to succeed in her career. It also means that she will be perceived by others as being 'together' and knowing what she wants.

Implications when Coaching Women to Lead

There is a tendency in many organisations to replace coaching with mentoring, particularly in younger managers: in our view the two activities are complementary and form part of the women-friendly organisation as shown above. When used alone, mentoring encourages people to become the same as those that are already there, i.e. usually more like the men in the organisation.

The best thing about external coaching for women in organisations is that it provides a support mechanism for them as a minority without losing their uniqueness. It provides the space to think that so many women living hectic (often two-shift) lives miss so badly. To some extent, coaching is the complement of the women-friendly organisation: it serves as a tool to build confidence, to trigger change and to think beyond established patterns and rules. In summary:

- Make coaching part of the core offering of the women-friendly organisation.
- Coach selectively but coach early, as part of a talent programme.
- Allow women more than one bite: coach at different career stages.
- Understand/advertise the leverage that coaching has on universal female experiences: confidence, networking, career management, work–life balance, etc.
- In 'immature' organisations that resist Positive Action for women or deliberate culture change, use coaching as a Trojan horse to increase women's presence on the senior echelons.

What is the global picture? Lessons from coaching women to lead around the world

So far we have looked at best practice mainly with a UK-centric eye, augmented by our experience of a large number of international clients operating from London. We now need to broaden this view.

• Women are hitting the same challenges in every country where they are pushing for leadership roles.
• The international shortage of leaders means that women have a role to play beyond their home base and need to understand context to be ready. At the same time, locally based coaches will increasingly deal with international executives.
• Best practice comes from everywhere. What are good ideas for designing better coaching interventions and more women-friendly organisations?

Women's status and human rights differ all over the world and this affects how they are treated in the workplace and the opportunities open to them. From those women venturing out into business in the Middle East to gender legislation in the USA and parts of Europe, recent social history has meant women have never been better placed to demand more from their working lives. We decided to look at how women progress at work in four different areas of the world: the USA, Europe (Norway), the Middle East and back to the UK. How does each country differ with its laws, policies and social mores? How does this impact coaching attitudes and approaches? In each case we start with a social and economic context for women using, as much as possible, comparable statistics for all countries. We then look at specific characteristics of senior women at work and how they are coached.

The USA

If you live outside the USA, chances are that you think the women's situation there is one of the most advanced in the world and that coaching has less need to be gender specific. The reality is more subtle. America is, indeed, a land of contrasts for women leaders.

Social context

We indicated in Chapter 8 that the US approach was one of Affirmative Action enshrined in law, most of which was drafted in the 60s and 70s, in contrast with the UK's preference for non law-binding Positive Action. The picture is further complicated by the fact that not all women are equal before the law: Black and Hispanic women face additional barriers as we shall see below.

So, what is the result of 30+ years of legislation? Table 9.1 gives us comparable statistics between the USA and the UK.

We therefore have an image of a fairly egalitarian society. This is confirmed by the fact that 37 per cent of women work in management, professional and related occupations. However, the USA is still a very unequal country, particularly in terms of pay. The USA was ranked 27th in the 2008 *Global Gender Gap Report* published by the World Economic Forum (Hausmann, Tyson and Zahidi, 2008) which, surprisingly, places it below most European and industrialised countries. In particular, the pay gap between women and men – 21.6 per cent – is considerable and higher than the Organisation for Economic Co-operation and Development (OECD) average. A slightly older study by the National Organization for Women (NOW) quoting late 90s data argues that: 'For every dollar earned by men, women on a whole earn 74 cents, African American women earn 63 cents and Latina women earn 57 cents.' If one remembers that ethnic minorities represent one quarter of the US population, then over 60 per cent

Table 9.1 Key comparisons between the USA and the UK

2008 estimates	USA	UK
Population above age 15	243m	50m
Of which actively employed	145m	29m
Proportion of economically active (aged 15+)		
Men	72%	70%
Women	60%	56%
Proportion of women economically active		
30–34 years old	74%	76%
35–39 years old	75%	77%
40–44 years old	77%	80%
Proportion of women in high leadership potential jobs (all ages) – includes legislators, senior officials, managers and senior professionals		
Men	17.9%	17.2%
Women	18.4%	10.7%
Women as a proportion of these roles	51%	38%

Sources: ILO, National Governments, WWS analysis.

of the population is receiving less money for the same job. Interestingly, the USA has never ratified the Convention on the Elimination of Discrimination against Women (CEDAW). Opponents have argued that it would relinquish too much power to the international community and force the USA to legalise prostitution.

Education seems to have no bearing on pay differences: in 2000, the median income for women with a high school diploma was $22,000 approximately, while men with the same qualification earned nearly $31,000. By the time they had Bachelor degrees women were earning $35,500 in 2000 compared to $50,000 for males (women earn 29 per cent less than men in both cases, although these examples do not control for job type).

In terms of influencing change, the USA had until recently a very low proportion of female senior government officials compared to other industrial countries.

Traditionally Democrats had more women in cabinet-level jobs than Republicans: a trend started under Jimmy Carter but accelerated by Bill Clinton. According to the Center for American Women and Politics at Rutgers University (CAWP), 56 per cent of White women voted for Obama: this commitment may well be rewarded as he has already appointed as many women in his first cabinet as Bush did over his full two terms. Very gradually the proportion of women at all levels of State legislature has trebled from 8 per cent in 1975 to 24 per cent today.

In contrast, there has always been a high degree of activism through advocacy groups and inside corporations. Women's networks are common in large organisations either on their own, or as part of a broader diversity agenda (including ethnic groups and gay and lesbian groups).

The same contrast between apparent equality and skewed reality can be found inside corporations: women represent 43 per cent of managers – one of the highest figures in the world. However, the same high dropout effect is seen as in other countries: in 2008 only 15 per cent of Fortune 500 board members were women, only slightly higher than the equivalent figure for the UK (11 per cent). We have tracked the numbers over several years and they are very sticky; despite efforts by companies to increase the number of women in senior positions, little has been achieved. Put simply, there is something very real holding women back from reaching the top in the USA. An interesting recent illustration is the *Financial Times'* Top 50 women in world business league table (2009): although the USA occupied the first and second position (both foreign women), it only offered 15 of the world top 50 female CEOs, well out of synch with economic weight, especially when UK companies boasted 7 and Swedish ones 3. Beyond the anecdotal, only 1.6 per cent of the CEOs of large American public companies are women.

Coaching women in the USA

So how do US coaches actually coach women to lead in the workplace? Most importantly, coaching women is taken seriously and has existed as an industry within the coaching industry for many years. In tandem, some of the major gender diversity agencies were first set up and operate from the USA, such as Catalyst. So the recognition that more is needed to be done to help women climb corporate ladders and for companies to retain their talent has been around for many years.

The North American coaching approach revolves around a combination of observation, assessment and conversation. The conceptual framework is generally non-directive, although there is much debate around this, particularly in the organisational arena. It may be a generalisation to say that US coaching is about the individual's power of determining his/her own success, but it is largely true. An interesting aspect is that the USA is the only country where telephone coaching represents more than half of contacts (different studies point to between half and two thirds of coaching being conducted by telephone).

With over a quarter of the population of a different ethnic origin and limitless cultural backgrounds, sensitivity to multicultural issues is important. A good coach is likely to have the appropriate subtlety and sensitivity to handle cultural differences. Reading up on specific background (e.g. statistics on Hispanics' achievements in Texas) is likely to be useful background information when dealing with career progression issues for example.

Otherwise coaches operating in the USA need to make provisions for expected cultural differences such as: a generally more proactive and materialistic attitude than in Europe; more rigid hierarchies in large businesses – despite the apparent lack of formality; the need to be seen to compete; and the importance of self-promotion. Many of these characteristics are not necessarily natural ones for women and can create another level of pressure to act outside their comfort zone.

The local expert's view

Dr Wanda Wallace, CEO of Leadership Forum Inc., focuses on women working in the financial services sector – one of the toughest areas in the world of work for women. For her, it is quite simple: 'improving retention (of senior women) requires improving management practices'.

Dr Wallace believes the main barriers to success for women in the financial sector lie in the fact that so much of the work is fleeting and transactional that it does not allow women to create strong relationships, particularly in client-facing roles. As she says, 'Women excel when they get to know someone well and have an opportunity to build a deeper connection'.

For her, women need 'good advice, good feedback and good advocates' to rise through the ranks and gain real business success. 'Peers and superiors often perceive women as lacking confidence, unable to relax and be themselves, difficult to get to know, not sufficiently strategic and not as able to use power effectively to engage the organisation', she adds.

Her remedy through coaching is to help women improve their ability to navigate competing demands, both within their companies and with external contacts. 'Build a strong coalition – people who can help you think about and position your cause – people who will support your strategy. Become astute to the political context in which you are operating. Recognise that you may be working in a tribal environment. In a sense, some managers operate fiefdoms, and the tendency is to hire like people. If women are to ensure that they and their work are valued, sometimes they need to tiptoe through the minefield; if you get too valuable to one tribe, another could oust you; stay under the radar and your worth will not be noticed. It comes back to relationship skills.'

She is also clear that women need to promote themselves better. 'Men do this well because they understand the need for it. Women need to learn to do it in an authentic way – not self-aggrandising or boastful.' Her top three tips for professional women to get on include:

- To be strategic – find out what that means in your company and strive to support that definition and gain the requisite experience.
- Confidence and presence matter enormously – cultivate both. One trait begets the other.
- Perfectionism can be both an asset and a liability.

Finally, when coaching women Dr Wallace urges them to recognise the downside of each behaviour and make a conscious choice about what is truly needed in a given situation. As she says, 'Sometimes an 80 per cent solution is the better option'.

All in all this is solid coaching advice, that would not be out of place in the City of London: a strong indication that women's coaching topics do cross the Atlantic, even if techniques differ slightly.

Norway

Of all the countries in the industrial world why have we picked one with a population the size of Ireland and therefore a small coaching market? Simply because it is, arguably, the most egalitarian country in the world and we wanted to find out if the need for coaching women using a specific set of approaches as studied in the previous chapters had reason to exist in such a society. We also wanted to study the effect of the law which fixed a minimum quota of women on the boards of public companies.

Social context

Northern Europe has always been well known for its equality and high standards of living through its long-term social policies. A high percentage of working women coupled with quality childcare has been part of the social fabric of life in Northern Europe for decades. This has been recognised with Nordic countries capturing the top four spots in the World Economic Forum's Gender Gap Index in 2008 (with Denmark a close number 7; Hausmann *et al.*, 2008).

Norway took the top position and is described as a 'haven for gender equality' by CEDAW. Here are some comparison numbers.

So the statistics are fairly clear:

• On the one hand an exceptional proportion of women's participation in the economy at all levels, especially during the years when leadership positions become available

Table 9.2 **Key comparisons between Norway and the UK**

2008 estimates	Norway	UK
Population above age 15	3.5m	50m
Of which actively employed	2.5m	29m
Proportion of economically active (aged 15+)		
Men	77%	70%
Women	71%	56%
Proportion of women economically active		
30–34 years old	87%	76%
35–39 years old	86%	77%
40–44 years old	87%	80%
Proportion of women in high leadership potential jobs (all ages) – includes legislators, senior officials, managers and senior professionals		
Men	10.5%	17.2%
Women	7.3%	10.7%
Women as a proportion of these roles	39%	38%

Sources: ILO, National Governments, WWS analysis.

(30 to 44). More specifically, of those women with children under the age of three, 72 per cent are employed; while 82 per cent of women work with children aged 3–6 (2004 data).
• On the other hand a participation in potential senior jobs that is comparable to that of the UK. This is because, according to the Norwegian Confederation of Business (NHO), jobs are still segregated by gender: women tend to work in the public sector – teachers, nurses – while men tend to occupy leadership positions in the private sector.

The good news is that, according to the Norwegian Stats Office (Statistics Norway, 2005; *Labour Force Survey*), 27 per cent of Norwegian women are tantalisingly close to our advocated target of one third women in middle management (public and private sectors). They also have a much lower drop-off rate compared to other countries with 22 per cent in senior roles (2005 data).

Norway has a high percentage of women serving as representatives on the Storting (Norwegian National Assembly). Some political parties have introduced gender quotas and in the Norwegian parliament and the municipalities, women occupy about one third of the seats. Gro Brundtland, the former Norwegian Prime Minister attracted international attention in 1986 when she formed a cabinet of which nearly half the members were women. Since then, a typical Norwegian Cabinet contains 40 per cent women.

Women directors in Norway

This strong position of women in public life has allowed the Government to draft specific Affirmative Action for women in management: since 2004 at least 40 per cent of directors on the board of state-owned companies have had to be 'of either sex' (i.e. women). This has been extended to all public companies in 2006. By Spring 2008 most of them had complied according to the Norwegian National Business Register – and the proportion of female board members had risen from 7 per cent in 2003 to 39 per cent in July 2008.

Naturally, there was widespread opposition from the corporate sector unimpressed at the State intervention. There was also great concern that there were not enough women trained and qualified to take on board responsibilities. This was partly solved by the main Business Federation of Norway setting up its own recruitment programme called aptly Female Future. Nationwide databases of women were set up and the National Public Investment Fund provides training courses around the country helping companies to find, recruit and train very senior women.

Today, able women are now visible at the top in corporate Norway – although many of these positions are in the state sector. Interestingly, corporate leaders now say that this was 'a necessary reform' and that they needed something to open their eyes to the talent they were missing out on. There is also a feeling that it was not that hard to find good women leaders. Businesses just had to look outside the men's locker-room and traditional male boardroom networks.

Obviously there have also been unintended consequences with the new law: many Norwegian women have a huge number of directorships, something that is not necessarily good for corporate governance; and Norway has imported so many directors from other Scandinavian countries that this has depleted boards of women in these countries! These complications are probably of a temporary nature and we are eager to see the impact of these new boards on business performance. Unfortunately, there are no data available for two reasons: one, it is too early; and two, there is no control group as all companies have had to change their board composition at the same time. A good summary of the experience to date is provided by Arni Hole (2008), the Norwegian Director General of the Ministry of Children and Equality in his report 'Government action to bring about gender balance': 'The lessons learned are certainly positive and serve both economic goals as well as democracy and fairness. Research has shown that diversity is good for a business' bottom-line.'

Coaching in Norway

Coaching is highly developed in Scandinavia (Sweden, Norway and Denmark) and it is suggested that the Scandinavian culture is the nearest to and most compatible with the ideals of coaching (Passmore, 2009). Interestingly, the Norwegian coaching market has probably reached maturity with 200 practitioners. In Norway, the cultural values of dialogue, good relationships and balance of interests in this region provide a positive setting for coaching. Our experience of working with Norwegian colleagues is that the Viking blood is never far from the surface: although they enjoy consensus like their other Nordic peers, they are equally comfortable in a good argument!

The local expert's view

Anne Solberg works with senior women in Norway. Although she thinks many good businesswomen would have broken through anyway, the 40 per cent women board participation law has created an urgent need for specialised coaching:

- filling functional gaps in business understanding to act as a good governor;
- finesse the ability to think strategically (locally and globally, have good competitive insight);
- dealing with conflict in senior teams/boards, team building, team dynamics; and
- managing commitments/pressure – good female non-executive directors are in high demand; one woman is reputed to have 15 directorships.

Interestingly, questioning values: 'Am I doing the right thing? What are the real values in my life?' and 'Is this meaningful to me?' is becoming increasingly important as women mature into their new roles. Although confidence and self-esteem play a part in coaching, it is not nearly so high on the list for women at work in Norway. This may be due to decades of equality in other areas, particularly economic/politics and childcare, and the fact that a high percentage of women have always worked and happily run children and family life as well. Anne cites other countries, particularly Spain, where this is not the case but where there has been a large increase in women reaching more senior positions. The difference for her is that many senior Spanish women choose not to have families mainly due to the Mediterranean/Catholic culture in which the role of motherhood alone is considered a desirable and possibly exalted position in society. (This is her view, we suspect it has more to do with Spanish women embracing contraception post-Franco.)

An interesting side effect of the new law is the impact on men and their coaching needs. Not only do they want help on how to cope with the influx of women at the top, but younger men – typically those aged 35–40 – now find themselves in a new age of equality with expectations that they will play an even greater role in family life. As Anne mentions, these are the men who have no role models. Their partners are high-flying women with whom they may compete in the job stakes, share joint childcare duties yet work harder than ever before, and still want a life outside work to be able to keep up fitness routines and interests. It is not only women who need resilience coaching, but often their partners as well.

Our impression about coaching in Norway is that the basics have been largely sorted out. Women still need specific coaching, but largely for the 'right reasons'.

The Middle East

We were intrigued by the Middle East: on the one hand the stereotype of Middle Eastern women was that they were not allowed to work; on the other hand we knew of plenty of examples of women of high influence and business impact in the region. Was there a two-level society? Could coaching flourish in the circumstances? Were issues even comparable with the rest of the world? We had to find out . . .

Social context

The first obvious distinction is the enormous range of women's conditions and freedom to work from the Levant to the Gulf. For this chapter we have not studied Turkey for example, where Güler Sabanci – whose family conglomerate turns over $15bn a year – has just been voted the world's no.5 woman CEO by the *Financial Times* (2009). We are also well aware that North Africa can provide in some cases a template for greater gender equality. For example Tunisia has recently opened up the political field, with women accounting for 15 per cent of the government and 27 per cent of the municipality boards. It also boasts that 40 per cent of its doctors are women, as are 70 per cent of its pharmacists. There is also a robust pipeline of women coming through: according to the *Arab Human Development Report* (UNDP, 2005), girls already outnumber boys in university enrolment in 12 Arab countries. In Egypt, they already represent 22 per cent of graduates.

For many years, visiting companies in Saudi Arabia could mean never seeing a woman in the workplace. In other countries and cultures, however, Middle Eastern women are finding ways to overcome past prejudices and are fast becoming modern business women of the world.

The labour laws in Arab countries are progressing, with many states guaranteeing women the right to maternity leave, prohibiting the dismissal or termination of the service of working women during maternity leave or pregnancy, and guaranteeing them the right to childcare leave and to a period for nursing babies. In Jordan, the law gives a male or female worker the right to take extended leave to accompany his or her partner if they have moved to a new workplace in another province or abroad.

However, the laws in many Arab states still penalise women who leave the home to work without their husbands' consent. Libyan law prohibits the employment of women in work that does not suit 'their nature'. Saudi Arabia has severe restrictions on women's right to work. The six constraining criteria have the effect of restraining women's employment mainly to the fields of female education and nursing. It also prohibits women from associating with men in the workplace. Some Arab nations also forbid women to work at night.

When it comes to pay, some states such as Iraq, Kuwait, Libya and Syria, explicitly provide equal pay for the same job. Yet others, such as Bahrain, have no legal provision for this at all. Qatar and Saudi Arabia stipulate equality in pay only in the civil-service sector.

How does this translate into quantified opportunities? We have used the United Arab Emirates (UAE) as a proxy for countries where women had relative freedom to work in senior roles.

The UAE's population is roughly the size of Norway's but the comparison stops here: women withdraw from economic life after having children and as a result only about half of the population is economically active. It is worse in other countries: according to the *Arab Human Development Report*, the overall female participation in employment across Arab countries is only 33 per cent. Also, fewer than one woman in five occupies a role where she has a chance to attain a leadership position. In business the road for women is usually that of family businesses. In the UAE, 30 per cent of small and medium businesses are now run by women.

Table 9.3 **Key comparisons between the UAE and the UK**

2008 estimates	UAE	UK
Population above age 15	3.3m	50m
Of which actively employed	1.8m	29m
Proportion of economically active (aged 15+)		
Men	93%	70%
Women	38%	56%
Proportion of women economically active		
30–34 years old	52%	76%
35–39 years old	48%	77%
40–44 years old	37%	80%
Proportion of women in high leadership potential jobs (all ages) – includes legislators, senior officials, managers and senior professionals		
Men	17.4%	17.2%
Women	4.0%	10.7%
Women as a proportion of these roles	18%	38%

Sources: ILO, National Governments, WWS analysis.

Empowering women through economic activity and education

The Middle East has not yet had a shock equivalent to what the First World War achieved in Europe and America: the right to vote and increases in the working population are direct consequences of global armed conflict and, later, contraception. The message is: if you get the work right, the ideological and societal changes will happen. There are still plenty of restrictions for women in the Middle East. In general women are denied full opportunity to participate in all types of activity outside the family on an equal footing with men. But there are openings, mainly through working in education/the public sector: for example, the EU has funded poverty alleviation programmes in the region; the EU speaks of supporting women's role, without referring to clashes between the genders, and sees it as a way to promote economic empowerment. Women in the workforce, and specifically in the public sector, can support women at home. Education is the other avenue: in the UAE, women represent a quarter of the workforce and 84 per cent work in education and supporting other women to become educated.

There are also women role models emerging from the region: Queen Rania of Jordan and Suzanne Mubarak of Egypt work tirelessly around the issue of women at work (particularly women setting up businesses), while Lubna Olayan is head of Saudi Arabia's Olayan Financing Group. Similarly, women's business networks have mushroomed around the Middle East and also operate at an international level with some based in the UK and USA. Finance seems to be a good path to high office for women in the Middle East: for instance Sahar El-Sallab is Vice Chairman and Managing Director of Commercial International Bank, the third largest in Egypt. In Saudi Arabia, Dr Nahed Taher started her career in major public sector infrastructure projects from water desalination, to metal mines, to airport terminals. She is now the first woman chief executive of Gulf One Investment Bank.

Coaching in the Middle East

With so much going on, and a new burgeoning workforce emerging in the shape of women, requests for coaching and training from women in management issues increase daily from this part of the world – and these requests are more often than not made to UK and US coaches. This can pose a dilemma for Western coaches in that their clients will happily speak in English, but it is always their second language. When coaching, particularly in terms of the important resonance and meanings put on words, care needs to be taken.

To understand the culture of each Middle Eastern country is also vital – each is very different and operates at different levels in terms of women's development and involvement in the workforce. A country like Jordan is far more advanced compared to Saudi Arabia, for example, where almost all the workforce are men.

Islam is also a fundamental part of most Middle Eastern

cultures – and as such is a powerful practice as well as belief for most Muslims. According to Islam, there is no divide between state and religion, or the personal or political. Muslims are expected to practise Islam well and it underpins and guides business and leadership styles. Generally speaking leaders expect to be obeyed and in return will look after employees and colleagues. Western coaches need to be careful they do not view these beliefs and styles of working and leadership as backward compared to the West.

Finally, another influence is the expat work style as many of the larger companies contain plenty of expats, and have done so for decades. Expat culture and behaviour will also form another part of the overall culture and have influence on the workplace.

However, when Averil Leimon was working with Women in Business International, with delegates from a wide range of Middle Eastern countries, it became clear that many of the issues women faced were universal – building confidence, balancing family and work demands and the guilt involved, overcoming prejudice and so on.

The UK

So we come full circle back to the UK. We have discussed a lot of the coaching context for women throughout this book. Now that we have had a look at three exemplar countries, how does the UK compare?

Social context

Like the USA, it traditionally has had significant gender gap in salaries (17 per cent difference between men and women in 1997 for full-time workers). This gap was significantly higher for both ethnic workers and part-time ones. According to the Low Pay Commission, 5.1m women worked part-time in 2008, representing 76 per cent of all part-time workers. The introduction of a minimal wage 10 years ago has helped part-time workers more than proportionally: today the pay gap is negligible for part-time workers (they tend to all be paid near the minimum wage) and only 12 per cent for full-time work. So is all well for women? Not quite: the pay gap accelerates dramatically with increases in salary, as seen in Figure 9.1. From the 75 per cent percentile of pay the gender gap grows to over 30 per cent. In other words women who are part of our coaching population will be paid typically one third less than their male counterparts for a comparable role.

This situation is also prevalent for our young women entering the workforce: although female students have significantly better grades than male ones (64 per cent high-quality secondary grades versus 54 per cent), in 2006 female graduates earned on average 15 per cent less than their male counterparts at the age of 24 – and this gender pay gap only increases with age, increasing to 40.5 per cent for women graduates aged 41–45. The UK's Equality and Human Rights Commission (2009) has estimated that it will take at least 20 years before gender equality in employment is a reality. One possible explanation is the choice of degrees: although girls outnumber boy graduates 54 to 46 per cent, women are more likely to study health, public services and care-related vocational qualifications, whereas men are more likely to choose to study vocational qualifications such as construction, planning, engineering and manufacturing technologies. Guess which job sectors are going to pay the most?

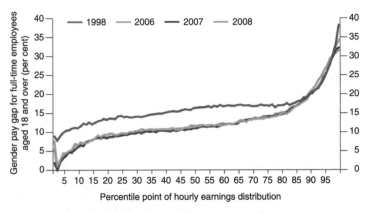

Figure 9.1 **Gender pay gap in the UK**

Source: Low Pay Commission report 2009

As we have already seen, in the UK, just 11 per cent of board directors of the FTSE 100 are women – despite at least 50 per cent of women joining these companies at graduate level.

Coaching in the UK

The UK, or European, approach is likened to 'in between the US and Asian' style of coaching by Jonathan Passmore (2009). In the USA, there is a highly individualistic coaching approach that focuses on the power of the individual to determine her own success. Asia, on the other hand, has a more collective attitude to coaching for which the individual defines herself via the group to which she belongs. The European approach seems to be mid-way between the two with a focus on individual power combined with integrated social and systematic thinking so group interests are also taken into account.

The local expert's view

For Dr Samantha Collins of Aspire, a UK firm focused on coaching women, the recession has changed what companies want senior women be coached about. 'It's all about performing better right now – and not so much about retention. It's getting the best from everyone and women are a key source of talent' (interview with Dr Samantha Collins by Helen Goodier, 8 June 2009). She mentions how coaching today is about playing to women's strengths and amalgamating them into the rest of the workforce. With women's attitude to risk in the banking industry, for example, there have been many suggestions that they can and do manage it better than men – given the chance. There has been plenty of information documented around this, including the view that if women had been directors of banks, the global banking crisis would never have been on the scale it was in late 2008. Logically, then, it is a case of helping men to take on more female skills – such as collaboration and teamwork – to create a new style of leadership.

When coaching senior women, Dr Collins is clear that

coaches need to be aware of the issues around women at work. 'Coaches need to understand the issues hitting women working at their level. They need to know plenty of the solutions; they need to be aware of the research that is coming out all the time on the subject and have a real understanding of the differences between men and women at work. On the latter, she quotes the example of men seeing their career as a ladder, while women are more likely to see their careers as a tree with lots of branches and the need to explore different paths, such as having a family and getting involved in the community for example. In her view, most coaching is about getting from A to B – or a traditional 'male' vision of coaching. 'With women, it is more complex than that – this model does not work – coaching women takes a more round-about approach.'

For Dr Collins, the crucial point in any woman's career is at management level around the age of 30 when good, well-qualified women are most likely to leave the workforce. 'Traditionally this is when women want both to start families and to be really successful at work as well. Usually at this level, women are overworked because they have no real power – they need help to understand what they want and what it would take, or what changes they can make, to make it work for them. This is where coaching can really help both with the individual to help her discover and make the right decisions, and companies to help them recognise that their policies and corporate culture may need to change if they are going to retain women and gain more senior women at the top.'

So coaching women in the UK according to this expert is pretty much as analysed in the rest of the book; her analysis of the post-crisis implications bring an interesting perspective to current work.

Implications when Coaching Women to Lead

So what are we to make of the different experiences of coaching in each of the countries considered above? And how does it influence our coaching of women in the workplace generally?

First, all women at work have a more difficult time than men, in whatever role and level they work. This varies hugely worldwide, and each country throws up its own anomalies according to its culture, religion and accepted behaviour to name a few – and these in turn affect psychological processes particularly to behaviour change, which ultimately is what coaching is all about. Interestingly, where major change has taken place in the workplace, such as Norway with its female director quota, the effect on others – particularly men – throws up other challenges that need to be dealt with.

Second, even in the countries that appear to give women the most freedom and where they can happily pursue their careers – the USA, the UK and Norway for example – there remain major issues around getting women to the top and retaining women at certain point of their careers, particularly in the late 20s and early 30s. However, if coaches help women to see that many of these issues are molehills rather than mountains to be scaled, women will be better able to achieve the behaviour changes that lead to success. Being able to help women navigate the labyrinth of the workplace, to find a way through to climb the career ladder – no matter what their culture or creed – is another aspect that affects women universally.

Finally, we should note that as the coaching profession becomes more established globally, coaches who are extremely experienced, particularly those based in the USA and Europe currently, will be approached to take part in more international-based coaching. Given that, it is useful to know and understand the full cultural setting for women in different countries before working with them as clients. What is more, useful models and coaching frameworks that work well in one country or culture may have their uses in others now and in the future – especially as countries develop and change.

10

Conclusions

In summary

So, there you have it. We started off with a potentially controversial question – 'Do we need to consider specific and different coaching for women leaders?' – and found that the answer is an incontrovertible 'Yes'. The business case is clear. Women represent a resource that if managed correctly would benefit the organisation, save companies from haemorrhaging high-quality talent, lead to the opening up of senior career opportunities for highly talented women and guarantee balance in modern organisations.

We found that to make a real difference, consideration has to be given to the working life cycle of the woman, often overlooked and misunderstood in our classically male designed and run organisations where life–work balance is given mere lip service. Women's needs vary at different career and life stages. It can all start to go wrong when women reach their late 20s or early 30s and realise just how tortuous the labyrinth can be. This is a high-risk time for loss of talent as shown in statistics and interviews. Good coaching, tackling complex, often conflicting performance and loyalty needs, will contribute to a real return on investment for the organisation.

Our research got to grips with what women really needed at each stage of their career confirming eight of the proposed key elements for success. While some referred to organisational changes, there were clear guidelines for coaching: networking, confidence, balance of career and family, career planning and development, and a clear understanding of strengths emerged as the foundations of success.

These findings were endorsed and illustrated with much humour, practical advice and honest opinion by the women we interviewed who were operating in the real world. As a result they provided the kind of role models they themselves had not had the chance to benefit from. This gives a better understanding of how coaches could proceed with women. Rather than just working to help women fit into a man's world, it became clear that there were specific areas which are likely to be of greater importance to women than to men.

Then, in our most practical chapter, we explored specific coaching issues, the relevant psychological underpinnings, possible approaches based on cognitive behavioural and positive psychology, and presented illustrative case studies to bring them alive. However, as women tend to be extremely heterogeneous, it was also clear that no one size could possibly fit all: at each stage of the work–life cycle different approaches and applications would be essential.

Our leadership review, while recognising that all core leadership interventions were just as applicable to women as men, discovered that for advanced leadership development, specific interventions had to be carefully considered and tailored in order for women to make the most of opportunities.

Not content to leave it all up to the women, we considered what it would take for organisations to be at the very least 'woman friendly' if not actually designed for the full range of human diversity. Coaching, inevitably, emerged as having an enormous part to play in facilitating organisational changes that can enable companies to retain their excellent women.

At a macro level, it seemed important to know what was going on in the world: how the issue was being resolved on a global stage. Cultural issues and stages of development notwithstanding, there were some clear indicators of worldwide change creeping forward and in some instances accelerating. There was also an enormous commonality in the issues that individual working women talked about the world over.

On reflection

There are key ways of stopping this waste of human capital.

Build a big house – for everybody

In the first instance we should be looking to build good organisations that take account of differences and give people the opportunity to live a full, satisfying and meaningful life – that is *all* people, not just women. Many men reach the end of their careers and express regrets about the insignificant role they played in their children's life or the superficiality of the relationships they had. Anything that improves the lot of women will in turn benefit men.

At all stages, men should be involved in the process. Good men do not even realise there is a problem for women. A senior banking client was asked to attend a women's award ceremony. With a wife, daughters and female pets at home, he was shocked by how uneasy he felt being hugely outnumbered by women and realised it was how senior women felt daily. That one experience changed his perception, understanding and way of running his business. We need more men to understand the issues and make change happen.

Spend your money wisely

Coaching needs to be carried out in the right way and at all the right times throughout the woman's work/life cycle. One of the challenges is that coaching budgets are often seniority related. This does not mix well with women's needs, which start in her late 20s. We advocate a comprehensive, client-centred talent approach. You do not spend all your marketing budget evenly on all your clients, why would you do it differently with your emerging leaders? Better to coach fewer people sooner than see them leave for the wrong reasons.

In the future?

Researching and writing this book has raised many questions for us, the authors. We want to watch this space with fascination, as we believe we are on the cusp of a tipping point to get more women into senior roles. We are also waiting with trepidation, as there have been false dawns before (witness the swings in the number of female partners in accounting firms for example). As coaches however, we know that backsliding is part of the change process! Here are some key themes to watch in the coming months and years – we will, no doubt, get involved.

The Role Models

We feel there is still a great need for women to have others they can look to for inspiration and encouragement. How can we bridge that gap while the numbers of senior women are still so low?

Generation Y

We only have a snapshot at present of their management characteristics but we know that this generation is different in a variety of ways, such as their acceptance of diversity, espousal of more classically 'female' attributes and desire to have a different lifestyle. Can they drive through a new way of working and maximise opportunities for change or will they sell out and just become 'another brick in the wall'? In particular, will *Confidence* be their biggest coaching issue or will this be replaced by something we still have to imagine?

Integrated Talent

Despite many companies' best efforts, coaching is still a disjointed intervention. What is the best way of creating client-centric approaches? We hinted at 'cafeteria' talent benefits that would include coaching. Will this become a reality?

And finally . . .

Overall, coaches have an enormous, instrumental role to play in creating a vast paradigm shift in organisations, one woman at a time. We need both male and female coaches (and supervisors) to be conscious of the organisational process and its effects on women, to understand the gender differences at work at every career and life stage and to have a clear understanding of the strong business and talent imperative at work.

So, let's get out there and make a difference!

The research

Questionnaire for *Coaching Women to Lead*

Hello,

This questionnaire is part of a research carried out to provide data for both a forthcoming book by White Water Strategies* (*Coaching Women to Lead*, to be published in 2010) and for an MSc dissertation on access to female leadership by a graduate student of the London School of Economics.

We are collecting experiences of women who started their careers in a large corporate or professional environment, made career decisions, and can reflect on what – if anything – has and would have helped them along the way.

This questionnaire is therefore aimed at women who started their careers in a corporate or professional environment with clear prospects for career progression. If this is not the case, please do not answer. Participation in this questionnaire is voluntary and anonymous, and answers will be used with discretion.

Some Background Information

1. How many years of professional experience (including graduate programmes and traineeships) do you have, as measured in full years?

---

* White Water Strategies is a leadership consultancy and one of the UK's top executive coaching firms.

Years

2. Do you currently work

   a) Full time
   b) Part time

3. Are you now:

   a) working in a corporate/professional environment (continue to question 5)
   b) no longer working in a corporate/professional environment (continue to question 4)

4. What do you do now?

   a) At work in a smaller company/firm/practice
   b) At work in your own/family business
   c) Complete change of profession (e.g. teaching)
   d) Other. Please specify:

Now please continue to question 6

5. Please choose the equivalent of your current level of employment:

   a) Junior management
   b) Middle management
   c) Senior management

6. In which industry/profession are you currently working?

About Your Career Journey

1. Looking back on your career, knowing what you know now, how well do you think you were able to take the important decisions that had a big influence on your career?

   Please give a score ranging from *1) I was completely in the dark and made a random decision* to *5) I had total clarity and I knew exactly which decision to make.*

   . . .

2. Which of the following *have* helped you in your career *in the past*?

Please distribute a total of 100 points to the options below, ascribing more points to options you consider more important. Please ensure that the total adds up to 100 points.

a) Better networking
b) Good role models
c) More confidence
d) Better career planning
e) Better knowledge of your own strengths
f) Easier balance of career and family
g) More systematic investment in your career development
h) Better understanding of the corporate culture

3. Which of the following *would have* helped you in your career *in the past*?

Please distribute a total of 100 points to the options below, ascribing more points to options you consider more important. Please ensure that the total adds up to 100 points.

a) Better networking
b) Good role models
c) More confidence
d) Better career planning
e) Better knowledge of your own strengths
f) Easier balance of career and family
g) More systematic investment in your career development
h) Better understanding of the corporate culture

4. Which of the following *would* help you in your career *at this moment*?

Please distribute a total of 100 points to the options below, ascribing more points to options you consider more important. Please ensure that the total adds up to 100 points.

a) Better networking
b) Good role models
c) More confidence
d) Better career planning
e) Better knowledge of your own strengths
f) Easier balance of career and family

g) More systematic investment in your career development

h) Better understanding of the corporate culture

Concluding Questions

5. Which of the following do you think would make women more likely to become tomorrow's leaders?

   Please distribute a total of 100 points to the options below, ascribing more points to options you consider more important. Please ensure that the total adds up to 100 points.

   a) Affirmative action at all levels
   b) A required quota of women on the board
   c) More open discussion of the topic
   d) Support from senior women
   e) Other. Please specify: ....
      ....

6. What do you think is or was the biggest challenge in building your career?
   ....
   ....

7. What advice would you give a younger woman who is at the start of her career?
   ....
   ....

8. Is there anything else you would like to add?
   ....
   ....

Thank you

Sample analysis and key results

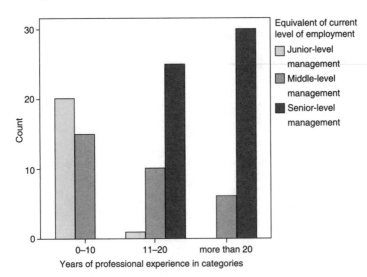

Figure A1 Respondents' profile: years of professional experience clustered by management level

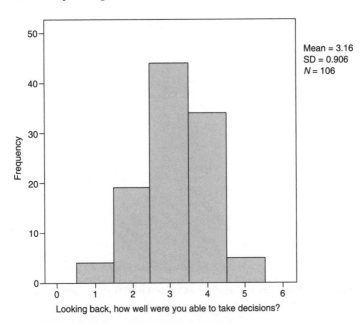

Figure A2 Question 1: frequency distribution

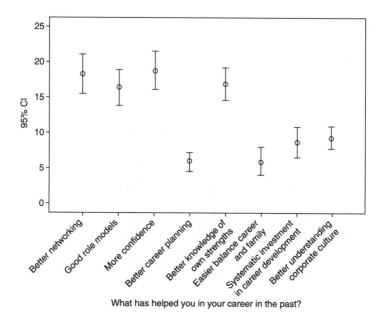

What has helped you in your career in the past?

Figure A3 **Question 2: distribution of 100 points illustrated at a 95% confidence interval (CI)**

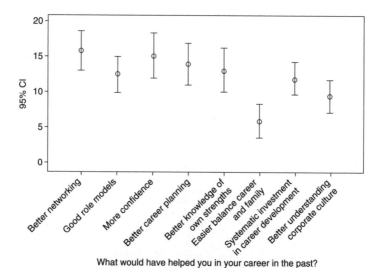

What would have helped you in your career in the past?

Figure A4 **Question 3: distribution of 100 points illustrated at a 95% confidence interval (CI)**

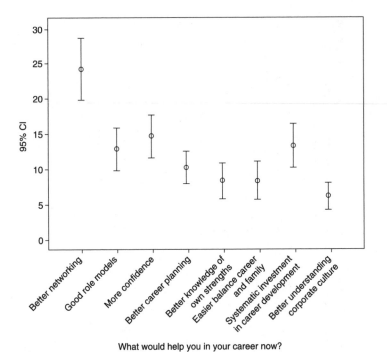

What would help you in your career now?

Figure A5 Question 4: distribution of 100 points illustrated at a 95% confidence interval (CI)

Results

Table A1 What *has helped* you in your career in the past?

	Networking	Role models	Confidence	Career planning	Knowledge strengths	Balance family career	Systematic investment in career development	Understanding culture
Mean	18.36	16.24	18.64	5.75	16.78	5.48	8.57	9.24
Median	15.00	10.00	20.00	5.00	15.00	.00	5.00	10.00
Standard deviation	14.69	13.91	13.61	6.72	13.09	9.91	10.636	8.90
Variance	215.72	193.34	185.18	45.19	171.35	98.21	113.115	79.13
Minimum	0	0	0	0	0	0	0	0
Maximum	70	60	80	30	60	60	50	50

Table A2 What *would have helped* you in your career in the past?

	Networking	Role models	Confidence	Career planning	Knowledge strengths	Balance family career	Systematic investment in career development	Understanding culture
Mean	16.03	12.62	15.28	14.14	13.22	6.08	12.13	9.51
Median	15.00	10.00	10.00	10.00	10.00	.00	10.00	5.00
Standard deviation	15.21	12.75	16.61	15.61	16.99	12.67	12.57	12.15
Variance	231.48	162.43	275.86	243.54	288.80	160.59	157.91	147.72
Minimum	0	0	0	0	0	0	0	0
Maximum	60	50	100	60	100	100	50	50

Table A3 What would help you in your career now?

	Networking	Role models	Confidence	Career planning	Knowledge strengths	Balance family career	Systematic investment in career development	Understanding culture
Mean	24.23	12.87	14.67	10.28	8.32	8.38	13.32	6.06
Median	20.00	10.00	10.00	5.00	.00	.00	10.00	.00
Standard deviation	23.52	15.77	16.07	12.72	13.70	14.70	16.43	9.88
Variance	552.94	248.76	258.15	161.71	187.71	216.13	269.77	97.70
Minimum	0	0	0	0	0	0	0	0
Maximum	100	100	100	50	100	90	80	50

Appendix 2

The interviewees

Here is the list of wonderful women who generously gave their time and their very forthright opinions to take part in this project and ensure that we were on the right lines. Three further women were interviewed but preferred to remain anonymous.

Alisa Swidler is a 37-year-old American ExPat with five children who has lived in London for the past eight years. She is on the Board of Save the Children, The One Foundation and Right to Play amongst others. By focusing on internment camps in post-conflict countries, Alisa has successfully organised the transport of vaccines and HIV medicines to an often forgotten population. She is currently working with President Clinton's Foundation in East Timor and Richard Branson's Foundation in Zimbabwe.

Baroness Morris of Bolton is the Shadow Minister for Women and an Opposition Whip. Previously the Vice-Chairman of the Conservative Party, she oversaw fundamental changes in the selection procedure to increase both the quality and the diversity of Parliamentary candidates. Before her parliamentary career, Trish was once a stockbroker. She entered the House of Lords in 2004. She is a devoted Bolton Wanderers fan. She is a mother, married to a judge.

Fleur Bothwick leads the Diversity and Inclusiveness agenda for Ernst and Young across EMEIA – 60,000 people over 87 countries. It is one of the most challenging and yet rewarding roles in her career to date and builds on previous D&I and HR roles in Investment Banking. She is a trustee of Working Families and the Tamasha Theatre Company and is a mother of three young boys, one of whom is autistic.

Gina McAdam runs Stratemarco, a London-based strategic communications consultancy, helping clients to 'tell their stories'. She worked in advertising, education and publishing in Manila, Madrid and New York before London, where she became Head of Marketing and later Head of Policy & Public Affairs for a national training foundation. In 2008 she won the Shine Outstanding Mentor Award for nurturing female talent in the hospitality and travel industry and is also a Director of Cafe Spice Namaste and Editor of *Profile Leader*. She has a 14-year-old son, Harry, who is her inspiration for everything.

Helene Martin Gee is Founder of leading women's network the Pink Shoe Club and a senior Parliamentary Adviser, including the All-Party Parliamentary Entrepreneurship Group, which she helped establish. An award-winning serial entrepreneur; she is also a Non-Executive Director and regular media commentator.

Jane Hollinshead is a Partner at Addleshaw Goddard in the Real Estate Group. She has experience in a wide range of commercial real estate transactions principally covering: commercial development and investment including advising on development agreements, leasebacks and future estate management structure, portfolio acquisitions and disposals of mixed user sites, acting on behalf of lenders in connection with the funding of both residential and investment and development sites.

Judith Hardy is Addleshaw Goddard's Director of Human Resources and a member of the firm's Executive Leadership Team. Her main areas of responsibility include HR strategy and culture change, performance enhancement, reward strategies and talent management programmes.

Kate Grussing had a classic fast-track corporate career until five years ago: from Wellesley College, LSE and Dartmouth to corporate finance and strategy consulting at Morgan Stanley, McKinsey, and JPMorgan. In 2005 she launched a boutique executive search firm that promotes senior female talent and flexible working. She has four children, a supportive husband and a passion for women's issues.

Kate Nash OBE is an effective disabled leader working strategically in support of long-term attitudinal and social systems for disabled people. A freelance consultant, she works with the business and public sector to help them become 'disability confident'. Her core product – consultancy in the establishment of Employee Networks is having wide acclaim. Her first publication *Disabled Employee Networks – A Practical Guide* was published in 2009.

Kate Turner is responsible for Specialist Advice (tax, trust, estate and financial planning) and two private banking groups (Professionals and Fast Track who look after young, high achievers) at Coutts. Prior to joining Coutts she had been working for Deloitte & Touche as a tax specialist dealing with private clients for 13 years.

Mara Babin is a founding member of MBMC International LLC, a consulting firm advising entrepreneurial companies. She is currently the Executive Vice President Development & General Counsel of AbilTo LLC, a web-based behavioural health company. From 1984–2008, she was a partner at Squire, Sanders & Dempsey LLP, focusing on the venture capital and private equity industries. She served as managing partner of that firm's London office for six years and created and led the European & Middle East Private Equity practice.

Monica Burch is a Partner in the litigation group at Addleshaw Goddard, one of the UK's largest law firms, and has sat on the board of Addleshaw Goddard since 2004. Her practice encompasses international litigation and arbitration.

Pascale Alvanitakis-Guelyis founder and CEO of Audentis Partners Ltd and Senior Advisor to Cogent Partners LLP, a leading specialist investment bank focused on alternative asset management. In her 17-year City career, she has worked at Arthur Andersen, UBS, and DLJ and was recently Managing Director and Head of Hedge Fund Banking at Lehman Brothers. An MBA from Aston University and an MSc from EM Lyon Business School, France, Pascale lives in London with her husband, Paul, and their two young children.

Penney Frohling is a partner at management consultants A.T. Kearney, where she leads its UK financial institutions practice. She has 25 years of experience working in financial services, having started her career at Citibank in the United States. She is the co-founder, with her husband, Dan Lonergan, of Gotham, a successful architecture practice and furniture showroom in Notting Hill which will celebrate its tenth anniversary in 2010.

Rosalyn Rahmé is an entrepreneur involved in Executive Search, Goldjobs, small businesses and people strategy consulting. International background with the motto 'people over process'.

Rosemary McGinness career started at Forte – but, having spent 11 years there, she joined Williams Lea and then spent four years in New York with Bowne Business Solutions. She jumped at the opportunity to return to Scotland working for a global business that was developing luxury brands such as upmarket Hendricks

Gin and The Balvenie and had enough foresight to put an HR director on its Executive Board. This meant that she has had the authority to build a strategic HR plan to attract, retain and develop talent from day one.

Sandra Kerr is the National Director for Race for Opportunity, which is a business-led network of organisations from the private and public sector. She is passionate about raising the profile of senior role models from diverse backgrounds. Before joining Race for Opportunity Sandra worked in the Cabinet Office advising Cabinet Ministers on diversity and policies on race, disability, gender, and work life balance across Whitehall. Sandra has also spent some years as a personal development and IT skills trainer.

Sandy Shaw is the Global Head of Middle East Private Banking at Coutts & Co. Her team, covering all major Middle Eastern countries, is one of the fastest growing and most successful areas within the Bank. Previously the Chief Executive, Private Banking at United Bank of Kuwait, she managed their two busy West End Branches, pioneered the introduction of the private banking concept into the Middle East market and personally oversaw UBK's professional handling of the Iraqi invasion of Kuwait.

Sarah Deaves is Managing Director, Affluent Banking, RBS UK Retail Division covering investments of all NatWest/RBS's 15 million customers and the banking of NatWest/RBS's top 600,000 customers. After joining NatWest in 1983, where Sarah held a wide range of roles in head office, marketing and general retail banking, 2002 saw Sarah become the first female Chief Executive of Coutts & Co., the UK's leading private bank. Sarah is a Council Member of Buckingham University. She has an MA in Geography and an MBA from Warwick Business School. Sarah won the Chairman's Award for Women in Business and Finance in 2006. She has two young children.

Sarah Jackson has been at the forefront of work–life balance campaigning since joining Parents At Work in 1994, Sarah is an acknowledged expert in the field. She led the merger, which created Working Families in 2004 and in recognition of her services to Quality of Life issues was awarded an OBE in 2007.

Sheila Duncan was appointed Human Resources Director in March 2009 at ScottishPower. Previously, she has held various roles in Scottish Amicable, Prudential Group and Royal Bank of Scotland. Sheila holds a Master of Arts (Hons.) from the University of Glasgow and is a Chartered Fellow of the CIPD. She holds a Non-Executive Director position on the Board of the

Scottish Huntingdon Association. Sheila is married. In her spare time she enjoys running, hill walking and high altitude trekking.

Sue Saville has spent her entire career within the banking industry, joining a local branch at 18 and undertaking a wide range of roles in the intervening 27 years. She is currently Chief Operating Officer of a business within a major bank's Corporate division.

Bibliography

Books and dissertations

Bandura, A. (1977) *Social Learning Theory*, New York: General Learning Press.

Bandura, A. (1997) *Self-Efficacy: The Exercise of Control*, New York: Freeman.

Davidson, M. and Burke, R. J. (eds) (2007) *Women in Management Worldwide – Facts, Figures and Analysis*, Farnham, Surrey: Ashgate.

Eagly, A. H. and Carli, L. L. (2007) *Through the Labyrinth: The Truth About How Women Become Leaders*, Boston: Harvard Business School Press.

Greenberger, D. and Padesky, C. A. (1995) *Mind Over Mood – Change the Way You Feel by Changing the Way You Think*, New York: Guilford Press.

Hewlett, S. A. (2007) *Off-Ramps and On-Ramps – Keeping Talented Women on the Road to Success*, Boston, MA: Harvard Business Publishing.

Kanter, R. M. (2004) *Confidence: How Winning and Losing Streaks Begin and End*, New York: Crown; London: Random House.

Leimon, A., Moscovici, F. and McMahon, G. (2005) *Essential Business Coaching*, London: Routledge.

Michaels, E., Handfield-Jones, H. and Axelrod, B. (2001) *The War for Talent*, Boston, MA: Harvard Business Publishing.

Passmore, J. (ed.) (2009) *Diversity in Coaching*, London: Kogan Page.

Sadker, D. and Sadker, M. (1994) *Failing at Fairness: How Our Schools Cheat Girls*, Toronto, ON: Simon & Schuster.

Walvoort, J. G. (2009) *Overcoming Barriers in Female Career Progression – The Importance of Strategies and Social or Individual Learning*, unpublished dissertation, London School of Economics, Institute of Social Psychology.

Articles, White Papers and reports

Adler, R. (2001) *Women in the Executive Suite Correlate to High Profits*. Pepperdine University. Available online at http://www.women2top.net/download/home/adler_web.pdf

Anon. (2007) 'New Arab women seek freedom to choose', AMEInfo.com.

Bandura, A. (1977) 'Self-efficacy: Toward a unifying theory of behavioral change', *Psychological Review*, 84(2): 191–215.

BBC News (2003, 16 September) 'Girls top of the class worldwide'. Available online at http://news.bbc.co.uk/1/hi/education/3110594.stm

Bell, J. and Huffington, C. (2008) 'Coaching for leadership development – a systems psychodynamic approach', in James, K. T. and Collins, J. (eds), *Leadership Learning – Knowledge into Action* (pp. 93–111), Basingstoke, Hants: Palgrave Macmillan.

Cadwalladr, C. (2008, 7 December) 'It's been a long journey and we're not there yet', *The Observer*.

Carruthers, J. (interviewer) (2008) *Voice of Experience – Wanda Wallace, CEO of Leadership Forum, Inc*. Available online at http://www.theglasshammer.com/news/2008/02/04/voice-of-experience-wanda-wallace-ceo-of-leadership-forum-inc/

Center for American Women and Politics [CAWP] (2008, November) *Women's Vote Watch*, New Brunswick, NJ: CAWP, Rutgers University.

Chambers, E. G., Foulon, M., Handfield-Jones, H., Hankin, S. M. and Michaels III, E. G. (August 1998) 'The war for talent', *McKinsey Quarterly*.

Clark, E. (2002, 31 October) 'Arab women lift the veil on business', *BBC News*. Available online at http://news.bbc.co.uk/1/hi/business/2356895.stm

Desvaux, G., Devillard-Hoellinger, S. and Meaney, M. C. (September 2008) 'A business case for women', *McKinsey Quarterly*. Available online at www.mckinseyquarterly.com/A_business_case_for_women_2192

Dezso, C. L. and Ross, D. G. (2008, 1 August) *'Girl Power' – Female Participation in Top Management and Firm Performance*, Robert H. Smith School Research Paper No. RHS 06–104. Available at SSRN: http//ssrn.com/abstract=1088182

Equality and Human Rights Commission (March 2009) *Equal Pay Strategy and Position Paper*. Available online at http://www.equalityhumanrights.com/legislative-framework/parliamentary-briefings/equal-pay-strategy-and-position-paper-march-2009/

Feltz, D. L. (1988) 'Gender differences in the causal elements of self-efficacy on a high avoidance motor task', *Journal of Sport and Exercise Psychology*, 10(2): 151–166.

Financial Times (2009, 25 September) 'FT top 50 women in world business, inaugural ranking'.

Fouché, G. (2007, 27 December) 'Quarter of Norway's firms face shutdown as female directors deadline approaches', *The Guardian*.

Gratton, L., Kelan, E. and Walker, L. (2007) *Inspiring Women – Corporate Best Practice in Europe*, Report, Lehman Brothers Centre for Women in Business, London Business School.

Gross, J. (2005, 24 November) 'Forget the career. My parents need me at home', *International Herald Tribune*.

Gross, J. (2006, 25 March) 'As parents age, baby boomers and business struggle to cope', *New York Times*.

Hausmann, R., Tyson, L. D. and Zahidi, S. (2008) *The Global Gender Gap Report*, World Economic Forum.

Higher Education Statistics Agency (2008/09). Information available online at: http://www.hesa.ac.uk/dox/pressOffice/sfr142/SFR142_Table7.pdf; and http://www.hesa.ac.uk/index.php/content/view/1578/161/

Hole, A. (2008) 'Government action to bring about gender balance'. WomenOnBoards; available online at the Women-omics website: http://www.women-omics.com/406-0-a-personal-account-of-the-quota-legislation-in-norway.html

Hopkins, K. (2009, 11 October) 'Women mentor male bosses as Dell joins push to smash glass ceiling', *The Observer*.

Hymowitz, C. and Schellhardt, T. D. (1986) 'The Glass Ceiling: Why women can't seem to break the invisible barrier that blocks them from the top jobs', *The Wall Street Journal*, 24 March, 1.

Ibarra, H. and Obodaru, O. (January 2009) 'Women and the vision thing', *Harvard Business Review*.

Kelan, E., Gratton, L., Mah, A. and Walker, L. (2009) *The Reflexive Generation – Young Professionals' Perspectives on Work, Career and Gender*, London: Centre for Women in Business, London Business School.

Marback, T. L., Short, S. E., Short, M. W. and Sullivan, P. J. (2005) 'Coaching confidence – an exploratory investigation of sources and gender differences', *Journal of Sport Behavior*, 28(1).

McKinsey & Company (October 2008) *Women Matter 2*, Paris: Author.

Nicholls, J. G. (1984) 'Achievement motivation: Conceptions of ability, subjective experience, task choice, and performance', *Psychological Review*, 91(3): 328–346.

Provencher, C. (2007) *The All-Weather Leader – A White Paper*, White Water Strategies Ltd. Available from info@wwstrategies.com

Ryan, M. K., Haslam, S. A. and Kulich, C. (2007a) 'Do women lack ambition: Explaining the opt-out revolution', invited address to SOM research fellows, University of Groningen. Groningen, The Netherlands, October.

Ryan, M. K., Haslam, S. A., Peters, K. O. and Kulich, C. (2007b) 'Opting out or pushed off a cliff? Examining gendered experiences to explain women's organisational exit', invited address to the Brisbane Symposium. August, Brisbane.

Sealy, R., Vinnicombe, S. and Doldor, E. with contributions from De Anca, C. and Hoel, M. (2009) *The Female FTSE Board Report 2009*. International Centre for Women Leaders, Cranfield School of Management.

Statistics Norway (2005) *Labour Force Survey*.

Swedish Business Development Agency [NUTEK] (1999) *Jämställdhet och Lönsamhet* [Gender and Profit]. Available in English at http://www.women2top.net/download/employer/key/genderandprofit.pdf

The Guardian (2008, 24 April) 'Live Q&A with Nicola Horlick'. Available online at http://www.guardian.co.uk/money/blog/2008/apr/23/liveqawithnicolahorlick?showAllComments=true

Towers Perrin (2007/08) *Global Workforce Study*.

Towers Perrin (2009/10) *Global Workforce Study*.

United Nations Development Programme [UNDP] (2005) *The Arab Human Development Report 2005 – Towards the Rise of Women in the Arab World.* Available online at http://www.arab-hadr.org/publications/other/ahdr/ahdr2005e.pdf

Databases and other sources

Catalyst, *Publications.* Available at http://www.catalyst.org

International Labour Organisation, *Statistical Databases.* Available at www.ilo.org/public/english/bureau/stat/info/dbases.htm

National Organization for Women [NOW] (1996). Available online at http://www.now.org/issues/affirm/talking.html. Statistics derived from Census Bureau and US Department of Labor.

OECD, *Publications.* Available at http://www.oecd.org/publications

UK National Statistics, *Publication Hub.* Available at www.statistics.gov.uk/hub/index.html

United Nations, *Statistics Division.* Available at unstats.un.org/unsd/databases.htm

Index

affirmative action 2, 46, 171, 181, 188
ageing relatives 107, 127
appearance 86, 141
assertiveness 69, 77, 97
authenticity 50, 74, 75

baby boomers 8, 10, 14, 20, 175
balance: career and family 40, 52,
    124–9, 200; gender 18, 169, 176,
    189, 200; work-life 47, 78, 81, 91, 97
Balanced Leadership 5, 36, 151, 152,
    156–63
behaviour: and culture 53;
    disruptive 112; gender 4, 43–4,
    49–51, 60, 135, 139; impactful 142;
    leadership 36, 80, 147, 161;
    practising 38, 108, 123
board of directors: career stage
    34–6; coaching 115–16;
    participation of women 16, 18, 20,
    24, 183, 188, 191; success factors
    61, 64, 68, 76, 79, 83, 86, 89, 96, 99,
    103, 106
body language 81, 140, 142–4
bounce back 78, 109, 130
brand (personal) 61, 67, 142, 178
British Minority Ethnic (BME) 101
business case 8–23, 84, 169

career: planning 40, 45, 56, 90, 173;
    progression 2, 26, 30, 53, 108, 151;
    stages 21, 25–39, 42, 179
child bearing 3, 29–32
Coaching Women to Lead: approach
    109–51; global lessons 180–98;

implications 23, 39, 49, 107–8, 151,
    163, 178, 198–9
cognitive behavioural 4, 153, 201
confidence: 4, 5, 23, 25, 31, 33–9, 40,
    44–5, 48, 50, 54, 62, 69, 70, 72–74,
    83–4, 110–16, 174, 179, 185, 200,
    203; and competence 111, 113,
    120
convention on the elimination of
    discrimination against women
    182
culture: company, corporate, et al.
    26–7, 38, 40, 47–8, 51, 53, 68, 69, 90,
    102, 138, 159; ethnic – see global
    lessons 180–98

demographics: and leadership
    supply 9–13; and impact on senior
    women 168–9
determination 64, 88, 98, 109, 114,
    125
diversity 16–19, 69, 86, 93, 169, 171,
    175–6, 203
domestic goddess 27, 34

education 24, 48, 53, 70, 90, 109, 152,
    160, 182, 193
emotional intelligence 32, 81, 154
engagement 13, 15, 113
equal pay act 166
equality: 36, 50, 101, 166, 171–2, 176,
    183, 186, 190–1, 196; racial 100
Essential Business Coaching 5, 152,
    162
explanatory style 111, 113–16

female attrition 21–3
femininity 50, 66, 71, 77, 80, 141
first 100 days 30, 140
flexibility 62, 68, 69, 72, 76, 81, 84, 90, 92, 109, 177
footsteps in the snow 121–4

gender: bias 108, 112–13; gap 35, 181, 186, 195–6
generation X or Y 13, 176, 203
glass: ceiling 66–7, 134, 176; labyrinth 3, 134–8
gravitas 38, 86, 141–5

happiness 51
homogeneity 124
human capital 202
husband 60, 66, 133, 192

internal locus of control 54
ITEA 5, 153–5

jigsaw 73

labyrinth – see glass
leadership 2, 5, 7, 8, 35, 63–70, 80, 97–8, 135, 152, 173–5, 180, 182, 187, 193, 201; cliff 3, 9–16; coaching 31, 36, 54, 122, 145–51; pipeline 21–3; rich corporation 16–20; see also Balanced Leadership, ITEA
Leadership Forum Inc 184
learned helplessness 54
legislation 72, 96, 99, 180–1
London School of Economics (LSE) 40

maternity 30–1, 60, 70, 72, 87, 167, 172, 191–2
meaning 30, 36, 56, 88, 162–3
mentors 26, 32, 49, 51, 57, 70, 74, 77, 80, 102, 105, 107, 172–3; see also footsteps in the snow
Middle East, coaching women in 191–5
multitasking 100, 109, 146

networking 5, 28, 30, 38, 43–5, 48, 51–3, 55, 61, 76, 86, 117–21, 170, 174–5, 200
networks: 32, 44, 48, 51, 55, 77, 80, 107, 110, 132, 173; women's 26, 28–9, 52, 62, 176, 183, 194
Norway, coaching women in 186–91

on/off ramping 3
optimism 26, 28, 39, 49, 131, 176
organisational dynamics 48, 51
ownership, taking 53, 74, 79

pipeline – see leadership pipeline
political radar 61
politics (organisational) 48, 51–2, 61, 68, 88, 106, 138
positive: discrimination 66, 166; psychology 54, 113, 156
power 65, 77, 80, 184–5, 197–8
presence 5, 91, 99, 110, 136, 140, 141–5
promotion 3, 25, 54, 56, 60, 71–3, 83, 114, 120, 146, 151, 178
public speaking 97, 156

queen bee 26–7, 71

reinforcement 103, 112
remote working 172
resilience: 5, 37, 70, 78, 84, 107, 130–4
resilient leader 157–8
retention 3, 9, 28, 185 – see also female attrition
role models: 5, 26–8, 32, 43, 48, 52, 55–6; interviews 57–109

salary differences 169
scenario planning 36, 160
self–belief 48, 77, 82, 94, 101, 107, 111
self–efficacy 111, 113
self–esteem 26–7, 31, 36, 38
self–fulfilling prophecy 115
separation anxiety 125
Sex Discrimination Act 166
sleepwalking 12–13
sport 78, 144
stereotypes 1, 49, 106
strengths: awareness/use 45, 50, 54, 77, 96, 99, 112–14, 118, 122, 131, 147; signature 162
stretch job 34, 169, 172–3, 177

talent: management 7, 89, 174; strategy 28; war for 8, 9

tipping point 7, 34, 79, 153, 203

UK, coaching women in 195–9
unwritten rules 26, 44, 79, 157
USA: 166; coaching women in
    181–6

variance analysis 41
visible 5, 156–7 – *see also* gravitas
vision: 37, 60, 79, 178; tunnel 131,
    154, 157

Volvo 174

well–being 51
White Water Strategies 41
woman–friendly organisation
    164–79
work ethics 43, 64

You Concept Car 174

zero based budget 170